KINGDOM
SPORTS

PROVERBS

THE DISCERNING ATHLETE

**A BIBLE STUDY FOR ATHLETES WHO
WANT TO LIVE AND LEAD WITH GOD'S WISDOM**

A 10-WEEK STUDY

RYAN LIMBAUGH

The Discerning Athlete: Proverbs

Cross Training Publishing

www.crosstrainingpublishing.com

(308) 293-3891

Copyright © 2022 by Ryan Limbaugh

ISBN: 978-1-938254-20-8

FOREWORD

I love the practical challenge and inspiration that comes from the mouth of God to us through the critical book of the Bible—Proverbs! Its emphasis on wisdom and godly living is invaluable for the coach or athlete. I have always reserved a part of my position meetings for sharing selected portions of Proverbs with my players.

Ryan Limbaugh has written this practical guide for athletes on Proverbs to help you understand and apply the Word of God to your sport. I trust you will be challenged and encouraged as you discover how to wisely live your life in everyday situations that include participating in sports.

It is our desire at Kingdom Sports to help train coaches and athletes to compete biblically by the power of God for the glory of God. We hope this study will help you understand how to transform competition so you will glorify King Jesus in every area of your sport. You can find many other studies for coaches and athletes at www.kingdomsports.online.

Ron Brown

Nebraska Football Director of Player Development

Co-founder of Kingdom Sports

www.kingdomsports.online

TABLE
OF
CONTENTS

DISCERNING ATHLETES . . .

DEDICATION

This book is dedicated to all the athletes who have pursued, played, and competed with wisdom. Thank you for having biblical discernment and passing it on to your teammates and to the next generation. Your fruit is evident in the lives you impact. Your reward awaits you in heaven.

INTRODUCTION

Divine Power for a Life of Discernment

In eternity past the one triune God, who exists in three distinct persons (Father, Son, and Holy Spirit), enjoyed perfect fellowship, love, harmony, and holiness. Nothing was wrong or empty. Everything was right and beautiful. But in an act of great love and with a desire to magnify His glory, He created the universe, this world, and His crowning achievement—humanity. He created man in His own image with a desire to be in sweet fellowship with humanity forever. He even gave man dominion over the earth to subdue it.

But man wasn't content to have sweet fellowship with God. Man wanted to be God. He wanted to take hold of God's glory and make it his own. This tragedy is revealed with man's interaction with the serpent in the midst of the garden. Man made the decision to walk away from the goodness and sweetness of God in order to test the waters of self-autonomy and independence from God. When he made that decision, he thrust all of humanity and the entirety of the world under the curse of sin. Childbirth became hard. Work became hard. Marriage became hard. Life became hard. Moreover, the ultimate curse of sin was eternal death.

But God, in His great love and for His own glory, was unwilling to stand idly by and watch all of humanity perish forever. He promised redemption. He promised a Redeemer. For hundreds of years, He made promises to man, established covenants with man, cared for man, delivered man, spoke to man, and demonstrated His love for man.

Then, all of a sudden, according to the eternal plan of God, the second member of the Trinity, the eternal Son of God, broke into human history and was born of a virgin—fully God and fully human. It was a miracle beyond our comprehension. Jesus Christ (Son of God—Son of Man—Fully God—Fully

Man) lived a perfect, holy, loving, compassionate life. He healed the sick. He raised the dead. He made blind people see and deaf people hear. He loved the unlovable. He touched the untouchable. He embraced the outcasts. He lived perfectly, loved powerfully, and served humbly.

He lived the life that you and I were originally supposed to live. And what did He get for it? Jealousy, envy, and hatred. Ultimately, He received torture and murder at the hands of sinners like you and me. But more than that, He was punished by God the Father as if He had lived the kind of life we have lived—lying, deceiving, lusting, bragging, cheating, hating, slandering. God the Father exercised righteous wrath on His sinless Son. Why? Because we needed redemption. We needed a Redeemer. So, "He made Him who knew no sin to be sin on our behalf, so that we might become the righteousness of God in Him!" Once the penalty for sin was paid, Jesus Christ cried out, "It is finished!" He died and was buried.

On the third day He rose from the dead, defeating death, sin, darkness, and hell itself. The victory was won, so that anyone who believes in Him will have eternal life, be in sweet fellowship with God, joyfully live for His glory, and experience His blessing. You can be rescued from the power, pollution, and penalty of sin and saved to the power of Christ's resurrection, purity of Christ's righteousness, and presence of Christ's glory forever. You can be indwelled and empowered with the same Spirit that raised Jesus from the dead. All you have to do is "confess with your mouth that Jesus is Lord and believe in your heart that God raised Him from the dead, and you will be saved."

That is the Gospel. That is the good news of salvation. If you believe it and have been redeemed by it, now would be a great time for you to pause and give praise to God and thanksgiving to Jesus Christ. Now would be a great time to offer worship to your Lord.

Some big questions still remain, however. What does the Gospel have to do with your life right now?

- What does that Gospel have to do with your sport?

- What does that Gospel have to do with your relationships?

- What does that Gospel have to do with your friendships?

- What does that Gospel have to do with your future?

- What does that Gospel have to do with your social media use?

The Gospel has everything to do with all of that! It gives you spiritual power and proper motivation to live and lead effectively for the glory of God. God's will is to work His Gospel truth into the very fabric of your heart so that you will be an athlete who possesses the power of God wherever you go.

I have written this study to help you be a discerning athlete in a culture devoid of discernment. Discernment is the skill of exercising excellent judgment in the situations of life. This world is desperate for discerning leaders. People need to be around leaders who know how to live wisely and make good decisions. Parents need discernment. Players need discernment. Coaches need discernment. So my prayer is that God will equip and empower you to be a discerning athlete who effectively navigates your life and leadership for His glory as you engage in this study of God's Word.

For our Discerning King,

Ryan Limbaugh

FORMAT

The format for this manual is pretty simple.
These are the component parts of each chapter:

CHAPTER TITLE

Summarizes the key concept in one word or phrase.

STUDY STARTER

Helps you understand the importance and relevance of the spiritual
truths you're about to study.

STUDY PASSAGE

Gives you the designated biblical text to read and study for the chapter.

STUDY HELP

Provides insight into the meaning of words, interpretation of
statements, and explanation of concepts.

STUDY QUESTIONS

Asks questions about the passage you must investigate and answer.

STUDY SUMMARY

Condenses the passage into one singular statement so you can understand the "big idea" of the text.

ATHLETE CONNECTION

Takes the Study Summary and transfers it to the world of sports so you can clearly see the Spirit-intended applications of the Word of God on the life of the Christian athlete.

KEYS TO WINNING

Guides you to meditate on the spiritual truths in the text and how they should shape your own heart and life as an athlete. Each key has a video guide found at www.kingdomsports.online.

GAME CHANGER

Points you to the person and work of Jesus Christ to help you be a discerning athlete through the power of the Gospel.

ONE BIG THING

Asks you to consider the most significant lesson you should take with you from the chapter.

IMPACT PRAYER

Motivates you to seek the Lord's help in applying the truths you have learned in each study.

STRATEGY

The strategy for this manual is quite simple.
This is our recommendation:

Recruit a group of athletes to walk through the study with you. These athletes do not have to be Christians to join the study. As a matter of fact, we encourage you to reach out to any and all athletes and leaders you think would consider participating.

Secure a copy of this training manual for every person who participates in the study. You can order more copies at www.crosstrainingpublishing.com

Appoint a leader for the weekly group study. This leader can be anyone with the ability and availability to lead. The key criteria are that this person is a Christian who understands sports, pursues Christ, and is willing to put in a little extra work to make the group study a powerful time in the Word of God. The group leader has the liberty to elaborate on the text and press into areas that are not necessarily covered in each lesson. This manual is merely a guide. There is freedom to take the study deeper and wider for more growth.

Schedule a weekly meeting day and time for 10-12 weeks. Allocate 45 to 60 minutes for the group study. Put the dates and times in your calendar and consider them high priority.

Invest 30+ minutes on your own prior to the study familiarizing yourself with the study passage, reading it, answering the study questions, and considering the Study Summary, Athlete Connection, and Keys to Winning. Go to the group study ready to participate, ask questions, provide insight, seek help, and sharpen your fellow athletes in their pursuit of Christ.

Encourage one another throughout the week with the truths you are learning. As iron sharpens iron, so one athlete will sharpen another.

Trust God to do a powerful work in your heart and life. The Word of God is living and active, sharper than a two-edged sword. It pierces to the division of soul and spirit, joints and marrow, and discerns the thoughts and intentions of the heart. It will do heart surgery on you if you will surrender yourself to it. So give yourself to this study and watch God work powerfully in and through you.

Read the Scouting Report prior to Week One. Just as you try to know as much as you can about your opponent before you play them, you need to know as much as you can about the context of Proverbs before you study it.

Don't worry if you can't find someone to study with you. The best way to profit from this study is with a group of other athletes, but you can certainly do it on your own. If you're a Christian, you have the Spirit of Christ living in you. He will give you illumination along the way. So don't let your isolation from other like-minded people discourage you. We encourage you to ask your local pastor, FCA staff, or church leader to walk through it with you. Anyone who loves the Lord and wants to grow into greater maturity could be a great study partner.

✦ ✦ ✦

SCOUTING REPORT

ON PROVERBS

SCOUTING REPORT ON PROVERBS

The TITLE of Proverbs

- The title reflects the literary style employed in the book. A proverb is normally a short, pithy saying intended to increase wisdom for life. Proverbs is a collection of discourses and sayings designed to increase wisdom in the person who fears the Lord.

The AUTHORSHIP of Proverbs

- Solomon is primarily responsible for the book's composition (ca. 970-930 BC). He is specifically mentioned in 1:1; 10:1; 25:1. We know that he was wise:
    - ~ He pursued and received the gift of wisdom from God (1 Kings 3:1-15).
    - ~ He was famous for his great wisdom (1 Kings 4:29-34).
    - ~ He composed 3,000 proverbs and 1,005 songs (1 Kings 4:32).
    - ~ He judged many court cases (1 Kings 3:16-28).
    - ~ He received international attention because of his wisdom (1 Kings 10:1-13).
- Others contributors include:
    - ~ The Wise (22:17-24:34)
    - ~ Agur (30:1-33)
    - ~ King Lemuel (31:1-9)

The AUDIENCE of Proverbs

- In the most literal sense, Proverbs is written from a father to his son (e.g., "Hear my son, your father's instruction and do not forsake your mother's teaching…"). Twenty-four times in Proverbs the writer says, "My son" (e.g., Be wise my son…).
- But just as Psalms was written as a songbook for Israel, the Gospel of Mark as a witness to people in Rome, and Colossians as an encouragement to believers in Colossae, they were all ultimately authored by God for our instruction and benefit. So each of us should be helped by the study, especially athletes who may be influencing other teammates in their formative stages of life.

The PURPOSE of Proverbs

- Proverbs is designed to instill wisdom in the one who fears the Lord, primarily by revealing the prosperity of a wise person's life and the pitfalls of a fool's life.

The STRUCTURE of Proverbs:

- Introduction   1:1-7
- Long Discourses on Wisdom   1:8-9:18
- Short Proverbs on Wisdom   10:1-31:9
    - ~ Proverbs of Solomon   10:1-22:16; 25:1-29:27
    - ~ Words of the Wise   22:17-24:34
    - ~ Words of Agur   30:1-33
    - ~ Words of King Lemuel   31:1-9
    - ~ Woman Who Fears the Lord   31:10-31

The STUDY of Proverbs

- Proverbs is a form of poetry. Poetry is compressed language; it says a lot in a few words. Therefore, we must read them slowly and reflectively, not speedily and rashly. No one should say, "I read all 31 chapters of proverbs this morning. I'm a beacon of wisdom now!" For this reason, we're not going to analyze every proverb in every chapter in ten weeks of this study. We will strategically study larger sections and individual sayings. The goal is to equip you for life-long enjoyment of Proverbs and application of its wisdom.

PREGAME QUESTIONS

1. When you hear the word "wisdom," what skills and abilities come to your mind?

_____

_____

_____

_____

_____

_____

2. Who is one of the wisest men or women you've ever known? List some specific ways he/she demonstrates wisdom and how his/her wisdom blesses others.

_____

_____

_____

_____

_____

_____

3. Wouldn't it be a shame if you can execute a great athletic move but could not make a big life decision? Wouldn't it be a huge miss if you could run faster but could not control your anger? Given the complexity of human life and the challenge of making decisions, what are two areas in which you would like to gain more wisdom? In other words, what are a couple skills you would like to add to your tool bag as you live your life and play your sports? Explain your answer.

_____

_____

_____

_____

_____

_____

_____

4. The title of this study is "The Discerning Athlete" because that is God's desire for you. He wants men and women who can effectively navigate life and leadership toward His glory. You have an incredible opportunity to be God's discerning athlete on your campus, with your team, and in your family. Will you write out a simple prayer asking God to make you a wiser, more discerning person through this study of Proverbs?

_____

_____

_____

_____

_____

_____

_____

5. If possible, choose another athlete to be your partner in this study for mutual encouragement, accountability, and prayer. You can hold one another accountable to do the pre-work, thoughtfully answer the questions, and implement the keys to winning in your sport. If you can secure a partner within the group, write his/her name down here and make a plan to communicate with him/her each week.

_____

_____

_____

_____

_____

_____

_____

_____

★ ★ ★

CHAPTER ONE
DISCERNING ATHLETES
VALUE WISDOM

**PROVERBS 1:1-7;
2:1-5;3:13-18**

STUDY STARTER

Today…

- An athlete will decide to click on a website he never should have.

    ~ That decision will ultimately ruin his life.

- A teenager will lie to her parents in order to hide the truth from them.

    ~ That decision will set her on a course of deception and manipulation.

- A man will hide some of his income to keep from paying his taxes.

    ~ He'll get away with it, but it will set him on a trajectory of compromise.

- A 13-year-old boy will decide to join a group of trouble makers to fit in at school.

    ~ That decision will stall his potential and maturity for over a decade.

- A Christian couple will raise their kids to be moral, but not worshipful.

    ~ That decision will make their kids conform to rules but calloused to God. They'll be great Pharisees for the rest of their lives.

Those things don't have to happen to you! Every hour of every day you are faced with decisions. Some small. Some big. Some even life-altering. You need to be equipped to make the right decisions for the right reasons in each situation. You don't need to have an appearance of wisdom without the real power.

The book of Proverbs aims at giving you real wisdom for your real, everyday life. As you work hard in school, hone your athletic skills, relate to your teammates, communicate with your parents, use the internet, and deal with life's temptations you need to know how to do so in such a way that brings God the most glory, you the most pleasure, and others the most joy.

God wants your character to be stronger, decision-making to be better, convictions to run deeper, leadership to be steadier, and worship to go higher. Real life is life with God. It's not simply making good decisions and instilling moral fiber into your life. It's pursuing the kind of life where you can have greater intimacy with God as you pursue His wisdom and righteousness.

What is wisdom? Wisdom is the skill to effectively navigate all of life toward the glory of God. Wisdom allows you to achieve the deepest worship, the most lasting joy, and the most profound influence on others. Let's dive into the deep waters of wisdom by studying key passages from Proverbs 1, 2, and 3.

STUDY PASSAGE

The PRIORITY of Wisdom 1:1-7

[1] The proverbs of Solomon, son of David, king of Israel:

[2] To know wisdom and instruction, to understand words of insight,

[3] to receive instruction in wise dealing, in righteousness, justice, and equity;

[4] to give prudence to the simple, knowledge and discretion to the youth—

[5] Let the wise hear and increase in learning, and the one who understands obtain guidance,

[6] to understand a proverb and a saying, the words of the wise and their riddles.

[7] The fear of the LORD is the beginning of knowledge; fools despise wisdom and instruction.

The PURSUIT of Wisdom 2:1-5

[1] My son, if you receive my words and treasure up my commandments with you,

[2] making your ear attentive to wisdom and inclining your heart to understanding;

[3] yes, if you call out for insight and raise your voice for understanding,

[4] if you seek it like silver and search for it as for hidden treasures,

[5] then you will understand the fear of the LORD and find the knowledge of God.

The PLEASURE of Wisdom 3:13-18

[13] Blessed is the one who finds wisdom, and the one who gets understanding,

[14] for the gain from her is better than gain from silver and her profit better than gold.

[15] She is more precious than jewels, and nothing you desire can compare with her.

[16] Long life is in her right hand; in her left hand are riches and honor.

[17] Her ways are ways of pleasantness, and all her paths are peace.

[18] She is a tree of life to those who lay hold of her; those who hold her fast are called blessed.

STUDY HELP

Proverbs 1:1-7

"proverb" = a wise message (i.e., saying) that is intended to produce greater wisdom in the person who wants to be wise. It is often a brief, pointed statement. It does not teach a universal truth, rather a general one. In other words, a proverb is not true for all people at all times. It is true for most people at most times. It's not an unconditional promise; it's a general statement of reality.

"Solomon, the son of David, king of Israel" = the third king of Israel, after Saul and David.

"know" = more than intellectual assent; it's a recognition and receptivity. Knowledge is more than the acquisition of information; it is having a relationship with truth. For example, there is a difference between knowing some facts about Jesus and actually having a relationship with Him.

"wisdom" = the skill to effectively navigate all of life toward the glory of God. The primary purpose of Proverbs is to impart wisdom. Wisdom is masterful understanding. It is skill, expertise in a variety of life's circumstances. Possession of wisdom helps a person cope with life and deal with the opportunities and challenges that are inevitable in life.

"...righteousness, justice, and equity" = The question Proverbs wants to ask you is not, "How high is your IQ and how many exams can you pass?" Rather, "how high is your spiritual discernment so that you demonstrate righteousness, justice, and equity in this unrighteous and unjust world?" Wisdom is not devoid of holiness, it's full of it.

"simple" = the inexperienced, naïve. The simple person is not a fool; he's just devoid of the knowledge he needs to be wise. The great thing about the simple is that he knows he needs wisdom, so he is very teachable. He doesn't act like he is proficient at everything. The sooner you admit to yourself and others that you aren't an expert at everything, the sooner you will learn from others and become wise. We are all simple and young in some areas of our lives. We all need help.

"Let the wise hear and increase in learning..." = Solomon understood a very important principle: Wise people never stop learning. They are always seeking to become wiser, more discerning, more skillful in the navigation of life toward the glory of God.

"the fear of the Lord..." = reverence for God rooted in a relationship with God that pursues the righteousness of God. It is the reverential disposition of the heart toward the glory of God. It is to voluntarily humble yourself underneath the Lord, acknowledge your dependence on Him, and understand that there is NO true wisdom without Him.

"...is the beginning of knowledge" = There is no true knowledge without reverence to the Lord. A really smart person may know how things work, but if he doesn't know why they work and for what ultimate purpose they work, then he may be really smart but also lack real wisdom for life.

"fools despise wisdom and instruction" = Some of the smartest people in the world are atheists. They are smart and innovative, but they are also fools! They don't see the big picture of life. They don't acknowledge the reality that everything is created by God, sustained by God, and that He is the all-wise, all-knowing God who imparts true knowledge. A fool is a hard-hearted person who rebels against the authority of God and resists the wisdom of God. Some of the most intelligent, visionary, successful leaders of our time have been fools. A person can be cool and a fool at the same time.

2:1-5

"receive my words" = Grasp my words, store them up. Don't resist them. Don't ignore them.

"treasure up my commandments with you" = Treat them as the greatest possible treasure, because they are from the Lord.

"making your ear attentive to wisdom"= bend your ear (an external act)

"inclining your heart to understanding" = extend your heart (an internal act)

"call out for insight" = declare your need for it (a humble act).

"seek it like silver" = actively pursue it as the most valuable thing you could find.

"search for it as for hidden treasures" = pursue it with urgency, as the most exhilarating and life-giving thing you could possess.

"then you will understand the fear of the Lord" = you will have the pulse of the glory of God. You will have a reverence for God rooted in a relationship with God that pursues the righteousness of God.

"and find the knowledge of God" = you will have an intimate relationship with the all-wise, omniscient God.

3:13-18

"Blessed is the one who finds wisdom, and the one who gets understanding" = In other words, "HAPPY is the one…!" In this context to be blessed is a personal and emotional state of peace, contentment, and exhilaration all in one. The wise person is able to say, "I'm at peace with God. I'm content in God. I'm exhilarated by God."

"Long life is in her right hand; in her left hand are riches and honor" = Long life, honor, success, wealth are things that people really want. The pursuit of wisdom will grant them.

"Her ways are ways of pleasantness, and all her paths are peace." = Pleasantness is delight, enjoyment, and excitement about life. Peace is completeness and wholeness.

STUDY QUESTIONS

1. What three things do wise people do (1:5)?

_____

_____

_____

2. Where does wisdom start (1:7)?

How should this shape the daily habits of a person who wants to be wise?

_____

_____

_____

3. The world often describes fools as unintelligent people, as if they lack the ability to make good decisions. But God describes fools in another way. He gets to the heart of folly by saying what about fools (1:7)?

_____

_____

_____

4. List the 8 action steps that a wisdom-seeker must take in order to gain the skill to effectively navigate life in this broken world (2:1-4).

_____

_____

_____

_____

5. What are the two rewarding results of those actions steps (2:5)?

_____

_____

_____

_____

6. List at least five rewards for gaining wisdom (3:13-18).

_____

_____

_____

_____

_____

_____

STUDY SUMMARY

Wisdom is the skill to effectively navigate life toward the glory of God. Wisdom is marked by prioritizing it, pursuing it, and enjoying the pleasure of it.

ATHLETE CONNECTION

As a discerning athlete who navigates your leadership toward God's glory, you will prioritize wisdom, pursue wisdom, and enjoy the pleasure of wisdom.

KEYS TO WINNING

▶ VIDEO GUIDE AT KINGDOMSPORTS.ONLINE

▶ PRIORITIZE WISDOM.

You have to want it if you're ever going to obtain it. Wisdom doesn't happen by osmosis. No person has ever looked up at the end of his days and said, "I have no idea how I arrived at this ability to effectively navigate my life for God's glory and others' joy." Moreover, there are plenty of good athletes who are not wise people. They mean well. They want what's good. But they aren't good with money. They lack good decision-making skills. They are imbalanced in their personal life. Why is that? It's because they haven't prioritized wisdom. They haven't marked out wisdom as something that's incredibly valuable to them. Wisdom starts with the fear of the Lord. The fear of the Lord is reverence for God rooted in a relationship with God that pursues the righteousness of God. It is the reverential disposition of the heart toward the glory of God. In order to gain your bearings on how well you prioritize wisdom, take this opportunity to describe 1) your current relationship with God, 2) how you revere Him, and 3) how you try to live according to His righteousness.

1. _____
2. _____
3. _____

▶ PURSUE WISDOM.

It doesn't matter how old or wise you are, you should always be learning and pursuing truth. I listened to a lecture on Proverbs in preparation of this study and the teacher said he knew a Christian man who was 93 years old. On his death bed the nearly 100-year-old man was reading a book on missions. Missions! The teacher said, "You'd think he should be reading a book on embalming or cemeteries. But he was reading about God's passion to reach the nations for Jesus Christ." That's wisdom. On the flip side, I recently heard a statistic suggesting that the overwhelming majority of people in the world stop actively learning at the age of 40. They just STOP! They put their heart, mind, and soul on cruise control. What a tragedy. The fact is if you want to be wise, you have to be a learner. You have to pursue wisdom in order to get it. You can do this in so many ways: reading and studying the Bible, listening to sermons, listening to spiritually edifying podcasts, participating in a book study, being in a weekly prayer group, etc. What daily and weekly habits do you currently have, or should you consider implementing to consistently pursue of wisdom?

1. _____
2. _____
3. _____

▶ ENJOY WISDOM.

The deeper you go in your knowledge of God, the higher you'll go in your worship of God. The deeper you go in your relationship with God, the sweeter your fellowship will be with others. The deeper you go in your reverence for God, the clearer you'll see the path toward His glory. So enjoy the ride! Enjoy the process of growing in wisdom. Enjoy spending time with God. Enjoy spending time with God's people. Enjoy opportunities for growth! God wants you to be incredibly happy as you humble yourself under His loving authority. So don't be anything less than what He wants for you. List three ways you have enjoyed the blessing of knowing God's Word and allowing it to shape your decision-making and leadership.

1. _____
2. _____
3. _____

Now pray a prayer of thanksgiving to God for giving you the blessing of wisdom.

GAME CHANGER

Jesus is the ultimate Game Changer when it comes to a life of wisdom. We need wisdom for a skillful life. We don't have it. But we find it in Jesus Christ. We need wisdom for a righteous life. We don't have it. But we find it in Jesus Christ.

Solomon was wise, but he wasn't sinless. He was wise, but he lost his way. Some thought he would be the king to usher in glory and power for Israel. Instead, the kingdom went downhill after his leadership.

But praise be to God that a true king, an infinitely wise king was raised up from Solomon's line. He sought wisdom. He taught wisdom. He embodied wisdom. He combated the world's folly with His wisdom. He resisted the devil's temptations with His wisdom. He led with wisdom. He loved with wisdom. He died with wisdom. Though the cross is foolishness to the world, it is the wisdom of God and the power of God! Therefore, we must first look to the person and work of Jesus Christ for a heart of wisdom, then we can look to the words of Christ in Proverbs for a life of wisdom.

The call to wisdom is first and foremost a call to faith in Jesus Christ!

ONE BIG THING

What is the most significant lesson for you to take with you from this chapter?

_____

_____

_____

_____

_____

_____

_____

IMPACT PRAYER

Father in heaven, You are infinitely wise and discerning. Thank You for loving us so much that You would reveal Your way of wisdom to us. Please help us prioritize, pursue, and enjoy wisdom so that we can truly lead others toward You. In the name of Jesus, Amen.

★ ★ ★

CHAPTER TWO
DISCERNING ATHLETES
TRUST IN THE LORD

PROVERBS 3:1-12

STUDY STARTER

As an athlete, you are part of a team! There are all sorts of teams out there. There are big teams and small teams. There are bad teams and good teams and great teams. There are selfless teams and selfish teams. I don't know what your teams are like, but I bet one of the things you don't want said about your team is that they are a collection of fools. I bet you want your coaches and all your teammates to have wisdom. That's why we are studying the chief book of wisdom in the Bible—Proverbs.

Wisdom is the skill to effectively navigate all of life toward the glory of God. Life is a journey. We are all on the way to somewhere. The Christian life is a journey toward the glory and grandeur of God. Wisdom is the skill to direct your heart, life, and daily decisions toward the glorious presence of our God and King, Jesus Christ.

Proverbs tells us one of the key attributes of wisdom is trust. Every person who has ever been wise has had a robust trust in the Lord. To trust is to fully rely on the integrity, strength, and ability of a person or a thing. To trust in the Lord is to fully rely on the integrity, strength, and ability of the Lord Jesus Christ. The Hebrew word translated "trust" in Proverbs 3:5 means to literally throw yourself down onto the ground, face-down, arms spread, feet spread, expressing to God your complete emptiness and utter need for His fullness. One theologian has said, "Trust is to do a belly-flop on God with all your sin and all your failure and all your fears." When you trust in the Lord, you stake everything on the Gospel-promises of God. So much so that if God fails, then you are damned. If God comes through, you are saved forever.

Do you remember the story of Charles Blondin? He was the famous tightrope walker of the 19th century. On June 30, 1859 over 25,000 people gathered to watch him walk 1,100 feet on a tiny tightrope that stretched 160 feet above the raging waters of Niagara Falls. He worked without a net or safety harness of any kind. He crossed over many times, then on stilts, then pushing a wheelbarrow, then with a load of cement in the wheelbarrow. The crowd erupted! He spotted a man cheering loudly and asked him, "Sir, do you think I could safely carry you across in this wheelbarrow?" "Yes, of course," the man replied. Blondin replied, "Get in." The man refused.

You see, there is a big difference between fascination and trust. It's one thing to be fascinated by a man who can do amazing things. But it's entirely different to actually get into the wheelbarrow yourself and trust him with your life. Trust is going "all in" with God. It's trusting His way, His plan, His character, not your own. Consider His trustworthiness for a moment. He made you. He sustains you. He gives breath to you. He blesses you. He helps you. He sharpens you. He teaches you. He forgives you. He never leaves you. He has secured an eternal home for you. If you want to be wise, then you must trust Him. This passage from Proverbs will call you to do just that.

STUDY PASSAGE

¹ My son, do not forget my teaching, but let your heart keep my commandments,

² for length of days and years of life and peace they will add to you.

³ Let not steadfast love and faithfulness forsake you; bind them around your neck; write them on the tablet of your heart.

⁴ So you will find favor and good success in the sight of God and man.

⁵ Trust in the LORD with all your heart, and do not lean on your own understanding.

⁶ In all your ways acknowledge him, and he will make straight your paths.

⁷ Be not wise in your own eyes; fear the LORD, and turn away from evil.

⁸ It will be healing to your flesh and refreshment to your bones.

⁹ Honor the LORD with your wealth and with the firstfruits of all your produce;

¹⁰ then your barns will be filled with plenty, and your vats will be bursting with wine.

¹¹ My son, do not despise the LORD's discipline or be weary of his reproof,

¹² for the LORD reproves him whom he loves, as a father the son in whom he delights.

STUDY HELP

In the Scriptures, God often gives instructions with incentives. An instruction is an authoritative directive, a command. An incentive is a motivation to follow the instructions that are given. "If you follow My instructions then you will experience these blessings." That's exactly what Proverbs 3:1-12 does. It gives instructions and incentives.

STUDY QUESTIONS

1. What are the instructions and incentives in vv. 1-2?

_____

_____

2. What are the instructions and incentives in vv. 3-4?

_____

_____

3. What are the instructions and incentives in vv. 5-6?

_____

_____

4. What are the instructions and incentives in vv. 7-8?

_____

_____

5. What are the instructions and incentives in vv. 9-10?

_____

_____

STUDY SUMMARY

Trust is going all in with God. It's trusting Him with all that you are and all that you have. If you want to be wise, then you must trust God's character, commands, plans, and discipline.

ATHLETE CONNECTION

Good athletes are normally smart, disciplined, meticulous, and intense with their sport. Because of that they often trust themselves and no one else. But if you want to be a discerning athlete, you must learn to trust God with all that you are and all that you have.

KEYS TO WINNING

▶ VIDEO GUIDE AT KINGDOMSPORTS.ONLINE

TO BE A DISCERNING ATHLETE THERE ARE FIVE ATTRIBUTES OF GOD YOU MUST TRUST:

▶ TRUST THE VIRTUE OF HIS COMMANDS (VV. 1-2).

> *¹ My son, do not forget my teaching, but let your heart keep my commandments,*
>
> *² for length of days and years of life and peace they will add to you.*

The son is instructed not to forget his father's teaching but to keep his commandments. It's easy to forget something when you don't treasure it. I can't remember my locker combination from high school. I used to know it by heart! Not now. Why not? Because I don't treasure it. It's not special to me. It holds no great value in my heart. However, I can tell you practically everything about the day that I married my wife. It was Saturday, August 9th, 1997 at 4:00pm in Anniston, Alabama on an overcast afternoon. The groomsmen wore black tuxedos. The bridesmaids wore yellow dresses. The church had stained glass windows with blue carpet and varnished wooden seating. I can remember many more details than that! Why? Because that day was the most significant moment of my life. I treasured it then. I treasure it now. I don't forget it.

Proverbs 3:1 is telling us that we will treasure what we love, and we will forget what we don't. Forgetfulness is the first step toward foolishness. If you want to become a fool, then start forgetting the greatness, faithfulness, and love of God. But if you treasure God's commands, then you will have a great quality of life and quantity of life. His commands are wise, good, loving, generous, thoughtful, gracious, and excellent. His ways are just, righteous, holy, and beautiful.

"Let your heart keep my commandments." True obedience is rooted in the heart. All other obedience is rooted in a disobedient spirit. Outward conformity with inward hostility is the recipe for spiritual disaster. The older son in Luke 15 had outward conformity to his father's instructions, but inwardly he hated his father. He just wasn't willing to be so audacious to spit in his father's face the way that his younger brother was.

We are tempted to disbelieve the virtuous nature of God's commands. We are often persuaded that God's way is not the best way, that our way is the best way. The world, the flesh, and the devil do a really good job at persuading us that God doesn't want our best. Sadly, we sometimes listen to those lies. So when we come to a crossroads between God's way and our way, we often choose our way because we disbelieve the virtuous nature of God's commands. And this is a huge mistake! God's way is always best. It is morally excellent and spiritually pure.

List two commands in Scripture that you really appreciate and how they demonstrate God's virtue and goodness.

1. _____

2. _____

▶ TRUST THE BEAUTY OF HIS CHARACTER.

> *3 Let not steadfast love and faithfulness forsake you; bind them around your neck;*
>   *Write them on the tablet of your heart.*
> *4 So you will find favor and good success in the sight of God and man.*

Here the father is speaking of the steadfast love and faithfulness of the Lord. In Exodus 34 the Lord says about Himself in third person, "the Lord, the Lord, a God merciful and gracious, slow to anger, and abounding in steadfast love and faithfulness…" God essentially says, "I am going to loyally love you! I will never leave you. I will never forsake you. No matter how many times you walk away from Me, I will never walk away from you. I will love you and never abandon you." And that is the exact same description right here in Proverbs 3:3! So we need to trust the loyal love of God.

Consider God's loyal love. When Adam and Eve distrusted God and walked away from Him, did God walk away from them and leave them alone? No. When Moses sinned against God, did God walk away from Moses and abandon him? No. When David committed adultery and murder, did God walk away from David and abandon him? No. Why not? Because God's character is made of steadfast love and faithfulness.

Give two specific examples of how God has demonstrated His steadfast love and faithfulness to you in the last year?

1. _____

2. _____

How can you practically bind His steadfast love and faithfulness around your neck and write them on the tablet of your heart?

_____

_____

What are some specific ways you can demonstrate loyal love and faithfulness to others so they can get a good glimpse of God's character?

_____

_____

_____

▸ TRUST SUPREMACY OF HIS WISDOM.

> *⁵ Trust in the Lord with all your heart, and do not lean on your own understanding.*
>
> *⁶ In all your ways acknowledge him, and he will make straight your paths.*
>
> *⁷ Be not wise in your own eyes; fear the Lord, and turn away from evil.*
>
> *⁸ It will be healing to your flesh and refreshment to your bones.*

We are tempted to trust what we feel and what we want, rather than who we know. We are hardwired to trust ourselves and to distrust God. We just are.

Consider the lyrics of Frank Sinatra's famous song My Way.

And now, the end is near. And so I face the final curtain. My friend, I'll say it clear. And I state my case, of which I'm certain. I've lived a life that's full. I traveled each and every highway. And more, much more than this. **I did it my way.**

Regrets, I've had a few. But then again, too few to mention. I did what I had to do. And saw it through without exemption. And I planned each charted course. Each careful step along life's byway. And more, much more than this. **I did it my way.**

Yes, there were times, I'm sure you knew. When I bit off more than I could chew. But through it all, when there was doubt I ate it up and spit it out. I faced it all and I stood tall. ***And I did it my way.***

I loved, I laughed, I cried. Had my fill, my share of losing. And now, as tears subside. I find it all amusing. Just to think I did all that. And may I say, not in a shy way. Oh no, oh no, not me. **I did it my way.**

For what is a man, what has he got. If not himself, then he has naught. To say the things he truly feels and not the words of one who kneels. The record shows I took the blows and **did it my way.**

That song has over 3,000,000 views on YouTube. People love it. But in reality, that song boasts in human folly. Consider the words of Proverbs 26:12, "Do you see a man who is wise in his own eyes? There is more hope for a fool than for him."

We often want to do things our way. But at the end of the day, we need to understand that God's way is best. It's always best. It's never second best. What are two experiences in your life where you had to trust in the supremacy of God's wisdom over your own? How did those situations turn out?

1. _____
2. _____

▶ TRUST THE PARADOX OF HIS PLAN.

[9] Honor the LORD with your wealth and with the firstfruits of all your produce;
[10] then your barns will be filled with plenty, and your vats will be bursting with wine.

This passage is a bit of a paradox. A paradox is statement that seems contradictory, but it is true. In verses 9-10 we would expect this, "Honor the Lord with your wealth and with the firstfruits.... and you'll have a little less in your barn and a little less wine in your vats, but in the end, you will have honored God and there may be something good for you in heaven..." But that's not what the proverb says! It says that when you honor the Lord with your wealth and give generously, then you will have more resources and more joy.

Consider the thought of being a server at Olive Garden. A big group of 20 people come in for a birthday party and you're the only one working the party. You take the drink orders and bring them out. You take the appetizer orders and bring them out. You take the meal orders and bring them out. You refill the drinks. You remove the extra dishes as they're used. You clean up a spilled drink. You're patient with a woman who is displeased with her dish. You run across the street to the local Target to buy some candles that the husband forgot for his wife's cake. You gladly serve this group of 20 for two hours. Then it's time for the bill. It's $493. The husband (who is serving as the host of the party) hands you five $100 bills, and then with a twinkle in the eye says to you, "Keep the change. You did a great job."

Do you feel honored or slighted in this moment? Slighted!!! You worked so hard, so diligently, and even went above and beyond the call of duty to make this birthday celebration special for these people. And you get a $7 tip for two hours of service!?!

Imagine how God feels when we give Him leftovers from our wealth. When we give a small portion of our paychecks, resources, time, and talent to the Lord's work we are essentially just like the man at Olive Garden. With a twinkle in our eye and a deceptively satisfying feeling of generosity, we are telling the Lord of glory, "Keep the change." And the reason we tell Him that is not because we want to insult Him; it is because we don't trust Him. We don't trust the wisdom, goodness, and faithfulness of almighty God to take care of our needs if we give generously of our first and our best. So we hedge our bets, protect our barns, store away what He has entrusted to us. This is a huge mistake! We think we're doing what's best, but in reality, we are doing what's worst. If we would just honor the Lord through glad generosity, He would increase the treasure He has entrusted to us. **Those who do good with what they have will have more to do good with**. Those who consistently give their first and best will receive more from God so they can give even more of their first and best. Trust the paradox of His plan.

Are there any adjustments you need to make so that you can give to God your first and your best? Consider these three areas of your life: time, talent, and treasure. Can you improve with giving God your time? How about your talent? And your treasure? Prayerfully consider that right now and write down what you feel led to do.

Time

_____

_____

Talent

_____

_____

_____

_____

▶ TRUST THE AFFECTION OF HIS DISCIPLINE.

¹¹ My son, do not despise the LORD's discipline or be weary of his reproof,
¹² for the LORD reproves him whom he loves, as a father the son in whom he delights.

This is the bottom line of the bottom line: Welcome the Lord's discipline! He loves you, cares for you, and is always working for your very best. So when He disciplines you He is doing it out of love.

God loves you so much that He sent His only beloved Son to receive divine wrath in your place. He is so passionate for you to have joy, happiness, and peace that He substituted His Son in your place. That is an unimaginable amount of love. So when He sends discipline your way, it is wise to receive it and learn from it.

When I was a sophomore in college, I was basically the captain of my baseball team. My coaches trusted me with various responsibilities. One week they went to the National Baseball Coaches Convention. Before leaving town, they sat me down and gave me the running, stretching, and agility assignments for the team. I was entrusted to carry them out. So the next day we got to the track to fulfill the coaches' requirements. But my teammates started to strongly persuade me in other directions. One of my teammates suggested that we play football instead of the boring running drills. The other guys latched onto this idea, even adding that we would get more cardio work from football anyway! Well, I happened to love football too and considered it a viable option at the time. I knew in my heart that this was not what the coaches had instructed. After some deliberation the decision was made. We played football and had a lot of fun doing it!!! No one was on campus. Who would ever know about this change anyway? The next week I got called into the coaches' offices. The first question I received was this, "How was the running on Friday?" My intentionally vague response was, "It was ok, Coach." He then said, "It's a funny thing. The tennis coach said she had to come to her office on Friday and looked up at the track and saw you guys having a lot of fun playing football. She was impressed by the team's enthusiasm." I got caught. I was wrong. I didn't lead well that day.

Some may say, "What's the big deal? What should the coach expect in that situation?" Let me tell you what the coach should have expected. He should have expected a young Christian man to follow the instructions of his authority. They were good, wise, and helpful instructions that would make us a better team. But instead of doing that, I rebelled and trusted in my own way and my teammates' way. I lost some of my coaches' trust through that experience. I was disciplined. But I gained a valuable lesson: "Be not wise in your own eyes; fear the Lord, and turn away from evil…" The fact is we could have done our stretching, running, and agilities and then played football! I was disappointed in myself and disappointed that I let my coaches down. But I learned a valuable lesson in that discipline. I need to do what's right no matter what kind of pressure I feel to do otherwise. And that lesson has served me well for 25+ years.

God's discipline is a sign of His love for you and a mark of His delight in you. It's not fun. But it is good, very good.

Are you aware of a situation when God has disciplined you? If so, what did you learn from that experience?

_____

_____

_____

How can you leverage your experience of God's discipline to help others when they have to experience discipline for their attitude and actions?

_____

_____

_____

GAME CHANGER

The Lord Jesus did perfectly what we do imperfectly. He fully trusted His Father's plans. He didn't doubt His Father's character. He didn't rebel against His Father's wisdom. He didn't run away from His Father's plan of suffering. Even when He looked down the barrel of divine wrath while He was in the Garden of Gethsemane, He fully trusted His Father, "My Father, if it be possible, let this cup pass from me; nevertheless, not as I will, but as you will."

Why would Jesus say, "not as I will, but as you will"? He knew the trustworthiness of His Father. The Holy Spirit bore witness to the Father's trustworthiness at the most pivotal moment in the history of the world.

Because Jesus has sent His very Spirit to live inside us and guide us along life's journey, we too can…

> Trust the Virtue of our Father's Commands.
>
> Trust the Beauty of our Father's Character.
>
> Trust the Supremacy of our Father's Wisdom.
>
> Trust the Paradox of our Father's Plan.
>
> Trust the Affection of our Father's Discipline.

ONE BIG THING

What is the most significant lesson for you to take with you from this chapter?

_____

_____

_____

_____

_____

_____

_____

IMPACT PRAYER

Father in heaven, You are infinitely and perfectly wise. Please help us to trust You with all that we are and all that we have. And use our trust in You to make a life-changing impact on others as we compete. For the glory of Christ, Amen.

* * *

CHAPTER THREE

DISCERNING ATHLETES

CHOOSE THE RIGHT PATH

PROVERBS 4:10-19

STUDY STARTER

We should all be preachers. That's right! Every single one of us should preach God's truth to ourselves every day. And once we preach it to ourselves, we should preach it to others as God gives us the opportunity. But it starts with preaching to ourselves. As I studied this passage, I began to preach it to myself. And then I began to incorporate the Gospel as I preached it to myself. Right now, I want to let you in on the message I preached to myself. It is rooted in Proverbs 4 and regulated by the Gospel of Jesus Christ.

Ryan,

There are two ways to live. There is a right way and a wrong way. If you choose the right way, life will be increasingly sweet and eternally bright. If you choose the wrong way, life will be increasingly wicked and devastatingly dark. So reject the wrong way and choose the right way every day until your final day.

But when you choose the wrong way, and you WILL choose the wrong way on more than one day, run to the One who never chose the wrong way and always chose the right way. Run to Him because He is the One who was crucified on that dark day as if He had lived the wrong way. Run to Him because He is the One who did say, "Father, forgive them for they know not what they do." Run to Him! Run to Him on your worst day and He'll love you as if it's your best day. Run to Him on your best day, because your best day lived in your own way will never be good enough on that Final Day. So Run to Him. And He'll not only justify you for that Final Day, but He'll strengthen you to live the right way every day until you see the full light of that glorious day.

That's the sermon I preached to myself as I studied Proverbs 4. In full disclosure, I doctored it up a bit so that it would sound nicer and have a little ring to it. But the bottom line is this: I know the best way to live is God's way. His way is the sweetest, wisest, and most rewarding way to live. But I have one major problem. It's this thing called sin. My sin keeps me from God's wise and righteous way. It keeps me from seeing His way, believing His way, wanting His way, and consequently living His way. So I need a Savior to rescue me from my blindness and folly. I need a Savior to rescue me from me! I need a Savior to guide me along God's good and righteous way every day.

Where do you want to go in life? How do you want to live while going there? What kind of example do you want to set for coaches and players who watch you? In this passage Solomon gives us two ways to live and the result of each way. We would be wise to listen to him and follow His instruction. He would say to us, "There are two ways in life: the way of wisdom and the way of folly, the way of life and the way of death, the right way and the wrong way. Those are the two ways. There is no third way." Let's study this passage with a desire to follow the God's way of wisdom.

STUDY PASSAGE

¹⁰ Hear, my son, and accept my words, that the years of your life may be many.

¹¹ I have taught you the way of wisdom; I have led you in the paths of uprightness.

¹² When you walk, your step will not be hampered, and if you run, you will not stumble.

¹³ Keep hold of instruction; do not let go; guard her, for she is your life.

¹⁴ Do not enter the path of the wicked, and do not walk in the way of the evil.

¹⁵ Avoid it; do not go on it; turn away from it and pass on.

¹⁶ For they cannot sleep unless they have done wrong;
they are robbed of sleep unless they have made someone stumble.

¹⁷ For they eat the bread of wickedness and drink the wine of violence.

¹⁸ But the path of the righteous is like the light of dawn,
which shines brighter and brighter until full day.

¹⁹ The way of the wicked is like deep darkness;
they do not know over what they stumble.

STUDY HELP

"Hear" = Listen to me. Don't ignore me. Fix your mind and heart on what I have to say.

"Accept my words" = Receive them and latch on to them. Just as a receiver catches a football and secures it all the way to the end zone, so should the son receive and secure these instructions.

"that the years of your life may be many" = I want you to enjoy a quality and quantity of life that surpasses that of a fool's life. I want you to know the sweetness of fellowship with God over the course of decades. I want you to enjoy the blessings of godly character over a long period of time. I want you to experience the joy of raising children and loving grandchildren for the glory of God.

"I have taught you… I have led you…" = A godly parent teaches his children in three ways: 1) formative instruction, 2) corrective discipline, and 3) personal example.

"keep hold of instruction" = Hold on to it tightly.

"do not let go" = Don't release yourself from God's wisdom.

"guard her" = Keep watch, protect, and preserve. You are a watchman on the wall and you will not let anything or anybody sneak in and steal God's wisdom from you.

"the wicked" = Those whose hearts are bent away from the glory of God and toward the glory of self. They are willing to do whatever it takes to achieve selfish goals. It often comes at the expense of other people's well-being.

"Do not enter" = Don't take a step toward it.

"do not walk" = Don't allow yourself to be led by the wicked onto their path.

"Avoid it" = Do whatever it takes to not go the wrong way.

"Turn away from it" = Go in the opposite direction. Don't hang around it. Don't flirt with it. Don't leave the door cracked so that you can walk through it at some point.

"pass on" = get going on your way, the right way. Don't look back.

"deep darkness" = Without the illuminating light of God's Word guiding their way they do not understand the cause of their problems. They don't see the connection between sin and death. They live in spiritual darkness. Our culture doesn't know why we have the problems we have. We regularly see mass shootings in our schools, malls, and places of business. We have an alarming number of suicides among our teenagers. Our culture does not understand why we can have the most money, the most technology, the most books, the most schools, the most doctors, the most medicine of any culture in the history of the world and yet have the least happy and most dysfunctional society in the history of the world. Our culture doesn't understand that. Why? Because, by in large, our culture has chosen the path of darkness instead of light. There has been a cultural rejection of God's light-giving wisdom.

STUDY QUESTIONS

1. In verses 10-13 what are the blessings of following the father's instructions?

_____

_____

_____

_____

2. In verse 13 "instruction" is given a feminine gender. Why is it so important to keep hold of instruction, guard her, and not let her go?

_____

_____

_____

_____

3. Verses 14-17 make it clear that the son should stay far away from those who do wicked things. Why?

_____

_____

_____

_____

4. What is so great about following the Lord's instructions (v. 18)? .

_____

_____

_____

5. What is so dangerous about hanging out with the wicked and following their way of life (v. 19)?

_____

_____

_____

STUDY SUMMARY

There are two ways to live: a right way and a wrong way. If you choose the right way, life will be increasingly sweet and eternally bright.

If you choose the wrong way, life will be increasingly wicked and devastatingly dark. So reject the wrong way and choose the right way.

ATHLETE CONNECTION

As a discerning athlete, you have an incredible opportunity to walk down the right path, avoid the wrong path, and help your teammates and friends do the same. Through formative instruction, corrective discipline, and personal example you can honor God and help others.

KEYS TO WINNING

▶ **VIDEO GUIDE AT KINGDOMSPORTS.ONLINE**

▶ FORMATIVE INSTRUCTION.

Wisdom is not the product of a one-time decision. It is the product of a daily commitment to walk on God's path. If you want to be wise, you have to commit yourself to God's path every single day. Formative instruction is teaching that helps someone understand truth. It helps form their thinking about a matter. Sadly, most athletes are not brought up with formative instruction about God or the Gospel. They know very little about the attributes of God, the plan of redemption, the good news of Jesus, or the way of righteousness. They may have heard a little truth here and there, but not enough to lay a solid foundation for a life of wisdom. As a discerning athlete, you have a great opportunity to lead your teammates in the way of the Lord. You can do this through integrating an FCA Team Huddle, recruiting a volunteer Character Coach, facilitating a player-led weekly devotional, and a host of other ways. I once had a coach who had a simple "Thought for the Day," in which he would take a couple minutes to teach us what the Lord had taught him that day. In today's anti-Gospel culture, you have to be very attentive to your authorities' demands on you, but with the Lord's guidance you can respectfully create a culture in which your teammates are being exposed to the way of wisdom. Take some time to consider how you already do that and some other ways you can incorporate formative instruction about the Lord with your teammates and friends (e.g. attending church together, leading a Bible study, listening to a weekly podcast, hosting a chapel service when you're on the road). Write those things down and make a plan to implement them.

_____

_____

_____

_____

_____

_____

_____

_____

▶ CORRECTIVE DISCIPLINE.

Corrective discipline is discipline that corrects wrong behavior and aims to shepherd a person's heart. "Whoever spares the rod hates his son, but he who loves him is diligent to discipline him" (Proverbs 13:24). Corrective discipline has two major goals – repentance and restoration. When you have chosen to walk down the wrong path the Lord is good at helping you get back on the right path. That is called corrective discipline. And corrective discipline is different from punishment! Punishment is punitive. Punishment doesn't have restorative, instructive, formational goals. But corrective discipline does. Corrective discipline's goal is to help you see where you are wrong and feel the emptiness of your bad choices. It is designed to bring complete restoration of the relationship you have with Him and others. So, when the Lord brings corrective discipline to you, it is a great act of love. It's uncomfortable for sure! But it's the best thing that could happen to you. Why? Because it will bring light to the darkness, life to the deadness, and hope to the emptiness.

How many times has the unity and success of a team been totally disrupted because the coaching staff and players didn't deal with a certain player's bad behavior the appropriate way? Too many times to count!!! As a player and teammate, you have the awesome opportunity to play a restorative role that brings real forgiveness, hope, and love.

This is a very basic example of how corrective discipline can happen in a way that is positive and formational.

Coach: What did I tell the team about skipping practices?

Player: It's not allowed.

Coach: What did you do?

Player: I skipped practice.

Coach: Was that the right thing or wrong thing to do?

Player: Wrong.

Coach: Part of my responsibility is to help you learn how to do the right things in life. Do you understand that?

Player: Yes sir.

Coach: I'm going to discipline you by sitting you out the next two games. At those games you cannot play, but you must dress out and serve your teammates by filling up their water bottles and making sure they are hydrated during timeouts. You will encourage the players with words of affirmation when they come to the bench. You didn't serve them by skipping practice, but this will help you understand the importance of being a good teammate. It will also send a positive message to your teammates. If you want to be part of this team you will accept this discipline and serve your teammates the next two games with enthusiasm. Do you accept it?

Player: Yes sir.

Coach: Also, because you wronged your teammates you must apologize to them before practice today. Are you willing to do this?

Player: Yes sir.

Coach: Great! Would it be OK if I pray for you and our team right now? I'd like for Him to use this in a way that makes us all better.

Player: Yes sir.

Coach: Let's pray. Father in heaven, I thank You that You're a God of forgiveness. I praise You for sending Your Son to die for the things we do wrong. Please help us use this situation as a learning opportunity. And please make us a better team because of it. In the name of Jesus, Amen.

Coach: I don't hold this against you. Now let's go have fun and get better today.

Player: Yes sir.

What is the difference between punishment and corrective discipline?

_____

_____

_____

_____

Have you ever been "punished" by a coach?

Have you ever experienced "corrective discipline" from a coach? Describe the difference (emotionally and relationally) between those two experiences.

*How can you promote discipline rather than punishment in your team culture?

_____

_____

_____

_____

▶ PERSONAL EXAMPLE.

The best and most effective way to intentionally influence your teammates is to live a life of integrity, serving, teamwork, and excellence. **The path of righteousness is caught more than it is taught**. The power of example is potent! When I was a kid, I watched my mom wake up at 4:30am on Fridays and drive to the church to cook breakfast for high school students so they could hear the Gospel at a prayer breakfast before they went off to school. Her love and sacrifice made an impact on how I live my life. I watched my parents treat one another with respect the entire time I lived under their roof. That made an impact on how I treat my wife. I watched my parents love their neighbors in sacrificial and generous ways. That made an impact on how I try to treat my neighbors. I watched my dad drive into housing projects and pick-up players on his baseball team, take them to practice, coach them, and stop by a restaurant on the way home and get them a burger so they could have something to eat that night. That made an impact on how I live my life.

I watched my parents in a thousand different ways, and they made a huge impact on how I live my life today. I don't have super-human or extraordinary parents. I have very human, ordinary parents. But the sheer power of their consistent example of sacrificial love trumped all the mistakes they ever made.

Never underestimate the influence of your lifestyle. Never underestimate the power of your daily attitude, language, or tone. It's not what you say first that counts. It's not what you say best that counts. It's what you say the most that counts. And what you say the most is the life you live every day in front of your family and peers.

List three character traits you would like to impress on every teammate that plays with you. Then list how you can demonstrate those traits to them on a daily basis.

1. _____

_____

_____

2. _____

_____

_____

3. _____

_____

_____

GAME CHANGER

It's sad but true. We all choose the wrong way at times in our lives. We get ourselves into huge messes because we walk down the path of wickedness. When we do that, we are not only making it hard on ourselves, but we are also offending the holiness of God. And an offense against a holy God deserves judgment. We all deserve punishment.

But Jesus came to save us from that. He came to fulfill the righteous requirements of God. He came to earth and never chose the wrong way. He always chose the right way. He walked the path of righteousness every hour of every day of His entire life. When we put our faith in Him, God imputes the perfect record of Jesus to our account. We get the righteousness of Jesus! He is the ultimate Game Changer. So run to Him with your sins! Run to Him with your bad choices! He will forgive you, restore you, and put you back on God's good path for your life.

Jesus saves you from a life that is wrong and strengthens you for a life that is right.

ONE BIG THING

What is the most significant lesson for you to take with you from this chapter?

_____

_____

_____

_____

_____

_____

_____

_____

_____

_____

IMPACT PRAYER

Father in heaven, thank You for showing us the right way to live. Thank You for warning us of the emptiness of the wrong way to live. Please help us choose the right way each day and to lead our teams down that same path. In the name of Jesus we pray. Amen.

★ ★ ★

CHAPTER FOUR

DISCERNING ATHLETES

WORK DILIGENTLY

PROVERBS 10:4-5

STUDY STARTER

Sovereign Grace Music has produced a children's album titled *Walking with the Wise*. It's inspired by life lessons taught in the book of Proverbs. One of the songs in that album is titled *Lazy Bones*. Consider the lyrics.

Verse 1

Have you heard about Mr. Lazy Bones?

You can find him sleeping on his couch at home

When there's work outside for him to do

He is working hard to find another excuse

Verse 2

Mr. Lazy Bones tells you he's afraid.

Never ever finishes plans he's made

When you want his help around the house

You can try to find him but he's never around.

CHORUS

Lazy Bones can help us see

What we never want to be

Doesn't have a hope or clue

When we work to please the Lord

God will make our plans secure

And He'll be glorified in all we do

Verse 3

See the busy ants working all the time

No one has to tell them how to stay alive

Getting ready for winter days ahead

Gathering their food until the time comes to rest

That song demonstrates the big difference between laziness and diligence. Your work ethic matters to God. Your attitude toward work reveals a lot about what you worship and prioritize in life. Proverbs 10:4-5 teaches us about work. Let's meditate on these two verses for a while and allow God to teach us a lesson about working diligently and how to transfer that lesson to those we lead.

STUDY PASSAGE

⁴ A slack hand causes poverty,

but the hand of the diligent makes rich.

⁵ He who gathers in summer is a prudent son,

but he who sleeps in harvest is a son who brings shame.

STUDY HELP

"slack hand" = The hand is the basic instrument of work. Most people work with their hands. Slack literally means loose, not tight. It is figure of speech that means lazy or negligent. A slack hand is a person who is lazy in his responsibilities.

"causes" = produces, brings about.

"poverty" = the condition of having little or no money, resources, or means of support. It is a deficiency of the basic needs of human life. It is inadequate food, clothing, shelter, health supplies.

"the hand" = the work.

"diligent" = literally, sharp. The word is used in Isaiah 41:15, "Behold, I make of you a threshing sledge, new, sharp, and having teeth; you shall thresh the mountains and crush them, and you shall make the hills like chaff." Figuratively, it means diligent. Which is to say "careful, excellent, precise, and thorough in one's work."

"makes rich" = The diligent worker doesn't become rich accidentally or coincidentally. There is a direct connection between diligence and wealth. The diligent worker produces wealth for himself and those who depend on him.

"gathers" = to pick individual crops from their place of growth and bring them all together into one group.

"in summer" = Summertime is harvest time. The fruits and vegetables were planted in the Spring. They grew and developed until they became ripe in the summer.

"a prudent son" = a son who demonstrates consideration for the future and concern for the family.

"sleeps in harvest" = falls into a deep, heavy sleep when its time to gather.

"a son who brings shame" = he acts shamefully and causes shame to come upon himself. Shame is disgrace brought about by one's actions. A young man who shuns hard work and embraces laziness is a disgrace to his family and to the people of God.

STUDY QUESTIONS

1. What causes poverty?

_____

_____

2. What causes wealth?

_____

_____

3. What does a prudent son do?

_____

_____

4. What does a shameful son do?

_____

_____

5. The word diligent means "careful, excellent, precise, and thorough in one's work." In your own vocabulary describe each of those words in a way that helps you understand the nuances of what it means to be diligent.

Careful _____

Excellent _____

Precise _____

Thorough _____

6. Shame is complex. Shame can be both an objective reality and an experiential feeling. In other words, you can **be** shameful, and you can **feel** shameful. A player can conduct himself shamefully but not feel an ounce of shame in his heart. On the flip side, a player can feel shame in her heart but not have a biblically legitimate reason to feel that way. Maybe she suffered an injustice and feels ashamed but did nothing wrong. How can you understand what is objectively shameful and what is not? In other words, how can you understand the distinctions between God's perspective on what is shameful and your own feelings of shame?

_____

_____

_____

STUDY SUMMARY

Diligent work produces wealth and honor, while laziness produces poverty and shame.

ATHLETE CONNECTION

As a discerning athlete, you have the God-given privilege to run from the emptiness and shame of laziness and pursue the honor and blessing of diligent work.

KEYS TO WINNING

▶ **VIDEO GUIDE AT KINGDOMSPORTS.ONLINE**

If you are going to be a discerning athlete who leads with wisdom, you need to know four realities about laziness and diligence.

▸ THE EMPTINESS OF LAZINESS.

A slack hand causes poverty,

If you are lazy in your work, you will bring poverty on yourself and those who depend on you.

I was a pastor for many years. During that time, I interacted with countless strangers who approached the church for financial assistance. Part of the church's mission was to help people in need. So I would sit down with them and ask them questions about their lives and circumstances. Sadly, many of the people I met were in poverty because they were lazy. They had a slack hand. But the fact is that our culture often encourages and rewards lazy people.

But lazy people are empty people. They are empty of motivation. They wake up in the morning with no drive. They are empty of vision. They have no goals for their life or their family. They are empty of worship. They have no desire to work at worshiping God. They are empty of resources. They have inadequate supplies for life.

Not all poor people are lazy people. There are millions of hard-working, honorable people who are poor and in need of financial help. But that's not the point of this proverb. The point of this proverb is to warn us against laziness.

Consider the words of the late, great Kobe Bryant, "**I can't relate to lazy people. We don't speak the same language. I don't understand you. I don't want to understand you.**" These are the words of a man who forced himself to make 500-1000 shots per day in the offseason! Kobe clearly felt strongly about the emptiness of laziness. He understood that laziness is a complete waste of a person's time, talent, and treasure.

Give two ways in which you have seen or experienced the emptiness of laziness:

1. _____

_____

_____

2. _____

_____

_____

▶ THE FULLNESS OF DILIGENCE.

but the hand of the diligent makes rich.

If you are diligent in your work, you will bring wealth to yourself and those who depend on you.

My grandfather (James T. Limbaugh) was a great gardener. His garden was always huge. It was about 50 yards long and 25 yards wide. He took great joy in tilling, planting, maintaining, harvesting, enjoying, and blessing others from that garden. I loved staying with my grandparents in June and July. My grandfather and I would go out to the garden together and pick tomatoes, cucumbers, and corn. We would get on our hands and knees and dig for potatoes. When we got a handful or so he would tell me, "Run these in to MeMaw and ask her to get them ready for lunch." An hour later we would sit down to a table of deliciousness straight from the garden: BLT sandwiches, homemade French fries, cucumbers and onions doused in vinegar, corn on the cob dripping with butter, salt, and pepper. It was nothing short of a summer feast.

My grandfather was a diligent worker in all that he did. As a decorated World War II veteran, he knew the value of life itself. Every day he sought to squeeze as much enjoyment out of it as possible. And he knew that a life of joy involved diligent work and the blessing of wealth that came from it.

Diligent people are full people. They are full of motivation, vision, worship, and love. They feel the blessing of life, the value of hard work, the joy of generosity, and the peace that comes from giving your all to God.

Peyton Manning once said, "**I never left the field saying I could have done more to get ready and that gives me peace of mind**." He prepared, practiced, planned, and work diligently as a quarterback. Consequently, he became one of the best to ever put on a uniform.

Give two ways in which you have seen or experienced the fullness of diligence:

1. _____

_____

_____

2. _____

_____

_____

▶ THE HONOR OF DILIGENCE.

He who gathers in summer is a prudent son

If you are diligent in your work, you will bring honor upon yourself and happiness to your family.

The picture here is of a young man who tends the family garden every day. He keeps his eyes on it. He exercises care, excellence, precision, and thoroughness in the upkeep of it. So he knows when he should pick every fruit and every vegetable at its optimal time. He knows that if he picks a crop too early, it will never develop into its full potential. He also knows that if he waits too late, its nutrients, taste, and value will be significantly decreased, if not destroyed. He knows that a small green tomato the size of a ping pong ball has been picked too early. He knows that a big orange tomato with cracks, wrinkles and flies has been picked too late. He knows that a red, round tomato that is smooth with a slight green tint at the top is perfect! You can wash it, bundle it, take it down to the market, sell it for top dollar, and help provide for your family everything they need for a life of worship and fellowship.

I once had lunch with an older man named Jimmy. To get to know him I asked him about his children. Jimmy told me all about his son. He got his undergraduate degree in international business. Then he stayed in school and learned the Chinese language and culture. He worked very hard, moved to China, and worked there for nearly 20 years serving as the CFO of major international companies. He has recently established his own company that delivers groceries to people's homes who have a hard time getting out. As Jimmy told me all this about his son's work he was beaming with pride. Why? Because his son is prudent! He is a diligent worker.

The most decorated college basketball coach in NCAA history is Coach John Wooden. He won more national championships than anyone in the game. With a resume that includes 10 titles you might expect that he was the person who coined the phrase, "Just win baby." But that is not the case. Wooden was much more principled than that. These were his words, "Success is peace of mind which is a direct result of self-satisfaction in knowing you did your best to become the best you are capable of becoming." I've read quite a bit about Coach Wooden. And one of the most surprising things I have learned about his leadership is that at the first practice of every season he would teach his players how to properly put on their socks and lace up their shoes so that they would not get needless blisters on their feet. Really?!? A big-time college basketball coach teaches his players how to put their shoes on?!? This is the mark of diligence.

Diligent work includes a joyful spirit, a zealous heart, a big vision, a selfless ambition, a creative mind, and a thankful disposition. Name two of the most diligent athletes or coaches you have ever been around and specifically how they worked in a way that blessed the team:

1. _____

_____

_____

2. _____

_____

_____

▶ THE DISGRACE OF LAZINESS.

but he who sleeps in harvest is a son who brings shame.

If you are lazy in your work, you will bring disgrace upon yourself and shame to your family.

Go back in time 3000 years. It's 1000 BC in the nation of Israel. Imagine a 21-year-old son whose parents have to take a trip in late Spring to visit their ailing parents. They entrust the entire farmland to their son. But without the accountability of his parents, he stays out late every night, sleeps in through lunch, and pays no attention to the crops. As a result, the family has the lowest yield they've ever had. When the parents get back from their trip, they find themselves completely unprepared to live through the Winter and Spring with limited food, money, and resources. What can we say about this young man? He is a disgrace to his family.

"There may be people that have more talent than you, but there's no excuse for anyone to work harder than you do." The Hall of Fame shortstop Derek Jeter made that statement, not only with his lips but also with his life. I don't know if Derek has ever read Proverbs, but I do know that his belief about the disgrace of laziness is spot on. Hard work is a non-negotiable character trait for those who know and love God. Laziness has no kinship to godliness. Laziness is shameful.

Laziness is a sign that a person wants physical comfort and personal glory more than anything else. Laziness is nothing more than an attempt to place oneself at the center of the universe and to tell everyone else, "Serve me. Love me. Worship me. Do everything for me. While I sit back and soak in the glory of my sloth."

Some athletes grow up in an environment of hard work. Diligence is exemplified, expected, and demanded. But other athletes are reared in an environment where they are coddled, babied, and pampered. Little is expected and even less is delivered. List three ways you can run from a disgraceful life of laziness and pursue a life of diligence with your whole heart.

1. _____

_____

_____

2. _____

_____

_____

GAME CHANGER

The Gospel is the good news of salvation through faith in the person and work of Jesus. The Gospel saves us from eternal punishment for our sins. But it not only saves us from death and hell, it saves us from a life of laziness and self-centered work. And it saves us to a life of self-sacrificing labor and daily diligence for the glory of Christ, the blessing of our families, friends, churches, and world. It saves us from sitting on the throne of our own little kingdoms and saves us to picking up a sword in one hand and a trowel in the other to be soldiers and servants in the building of His kingdom.

Jesus is the ultimate Game Changer when it comes to working diligently. Why? Because He provides the greatest power, motivation, and example to roll up our sleeves each day and give all that we have and all that we are for His glory.

ONE BIG THING

What is the most significant lesson for you to take with you from this chapter?

_____

_____

_____

_____

_____

_____

_____

_____

IMPACT PRAYER

Father in heaven, thank You for Your Son's hard work for our salvation. Thank You for His diligence to toil, serve, teach, work, love, and bless everyone around Him. Please help us fight against the temptation toward laziness and to follow His great example of diligence. For the glory of Your great name, Amen.

NOTES

★ ★ ★

CHAPTER FIVE
DISCERNING ATHLETES
SPEAK WORDS OF LIFE

PROVERBS 10:18-21

STUDY STARTER

At one time we were all at enmity with God. We were rebels against His authority. We rejected His goodness. We disobeyed His pure and perfect will. We lived according to our own standards and in pursuit of our own glory. That was who we were before we became Christians. We were blind to His glory, deaf to His message of love, and dead in our sins. And then, in an amazing turn of events, God opened our blind eyes and caused us to see the glory of Jesus Christ. He unclogged our deaf ears and caused us to hear and rejoice in the message of the cross. He awakened our dead hearts and caused us to feel the power of His Gospel love. He made us see. He made us hear. He made us alive.

But that's not all He did. He made us His messengers, His ambassadors! 2 Corinthians 5 tells us that God has given to us the ministry of reconciliation and the message of reconciliation. We are ambassadors for Christ. God is making His appeal through us. You see, God has not only transformed your eyes so that you can see Christ, your ears so that you can hear Christ, and your heart so that you can love Christ. He is in the business of transforming your mouth, so that you can speak of the greatness of Christ. The chief responsibility of an ambassador is to speak the message of the King. And if you're a Christian, that's what you are called to do every day of your life. Your privilege and responsibility is to communicate in a way that accurately represents who your King is. In so doing, you will effectively influence people to worship and serve Him.

Now sometimes as Christians we have a tendency to get a little carried away with this responsibility. We don't understand it exactly. And we apply it in a not-so-wise way. We think if we can quote enough Scripture to people, then we will be good ambassadors. Consider a fictitious example of a man and his wife. We will call them Stuart and Stephanie. They are both new Christians. Stuart is taking this responsibility of ambassadorship very seriously.

> Stephanie: "Good morning honey."
> Stuart: "Sing praises to the Lord, O you His saints, and give thanks to His holy name…. Weeping may tarry for the night, but joy comes in the morning."
> Stephanie: "Can I make you a piece of toast?"

Stuart: "Man shall not live by bread alone, but by every Word that proceeds from the mouth of God."

Stephanie: "Have a great day!"

Stuart: "This is the day that the Lord has made. Let us rejoice and be glad in it."

Stephanie: "I love you."

Stuart (as he drives off): "Love is patient. Love is kind. Love does not envy or boast. It is not arrogant or rude…"

Stephanie (later in the day) texts: "Can you stop by the grocery store and pick-up onions and potatoes?"

Stuart texts back: "All things are lawful for me but not all things are helpful. Food is for the stomach and the stomach for food. God will destroy both one and the other."

Stephanie texts: "What are our Saturday plans?"

Stuart responds: "Honor the Sabbath day and keep it holy."

Stephanie: "What are we going to do about Stuart Jr.'s failing grade in Algebra?"

Stuart: "Train up a child in the way he should go, and in the end, he will not depart from it."

That kind of communication could get really frustrating really fast for Stephanie! **Speaking as an ambassador for Christ is not so much about quoting biblical words, as it is about speaking with a biblical agenda**. It's not so much about reciting Scripture, as it is embodying the character of Scripture and communicating the love of God.

Let's study Proverbs 10:18-21 with a strong desire to learn how to speak as God's messengers.

STUDY PASSAGE

[18] The one who conceals hatred has lying lips,

and whoever utters slander is a fool.

[19] When words are many, transgression is not lacking,

but whoever restrains his lips is prudent.

[20] The tongue of the righteous is choice silver;

the heart of the wicked is of little worth.

[21] The lips of the righteous feed many,

but fools die for lack of sense.

STUDY HELP

"conceals" = covers, hides.

"utters slander" = the communication of false charges or needless negative information that disparage a person's character.

"transgression" = sin.

"restrains" = holds back.

"prudent" = one who shows thoughtfulness, care, and concern for the future.

STUDY QUESTIONS

1. What motives would a person have to conceal hatred?

_____

_____

_____

_____

2. Why is it foolish to utter slander?

_____

_____

_____

_____

3. Why is it dangerous to talk incessantly?

_____

_____

_____

_____

4. The righteous person's speech is described as choice silver, which implies that it is extremely valuable. Do you know someone whose communication is very valuable to you? If so, what makes that person's speech so valuable?

_____

_____

_____

_____

5. **"The lips of the righteous feed many."** Elaborate on how this truth is played out in everyday life.

_____

_____

_____

_____

6. Describe a time when you have been nourished by another person's words.

_____

_____

_____

_____

STUDY SUMMARY

A wise person understands that the chief function of an ambassador is to speak the message of the King. The Christian's privilege is to communicate in such a way that accurately represents the purity, love, grace, and truth of Jesus. In so doing, others will be influenced to worship and serve Him.

ATHLETE CONNECTION

As a discerning athlete you will embrace your role as an ambassador of King Jesus. Your communication will not be marked by the slander and malice of this world but by the love and hope of the King. As a result, your circle of influence will be nourished and blessed.

KEYS TO WINNING

▶ **VIDEO GUIDE AT KINGDOMSPORTS.ONLINE**

▶ DON'T HAVE HONEY ON YOUR LIPS WITH HATRED IN YOUR HEART.

"The one who conceals hatred has lying lips."

The person who has hatred in his heart for someone, and does not deal with that hatred, but instead interacts with that person as if he loves him, is a liar. He deceives that person by the way he acts toward him and speaks to him.

If your speech contradicts your heart, then you are a liar.

When you hate a person but pretend that you love that person, then you are building a relationship on a lie.

I once had a man approach me after a church service and tell me he had held a grudge against me for two solid years. He didn't like me. He wasn't for me. He got angry with me at some point and just set his heart against me. I was completely unaware of it. After a couple years of being in church together every Sunday and every Wednesday, eating meals together, and serving on leadership teams together, he came and admitted this to me and asked for my forgiveness. It's good that he admitted it. But it's sad that we "fellowshipped" together for two years while he concealed his hatred toward me.

The relationship we had was not real fellowship. It was fake fellowship that was built and sustained on hidden anger. Come to find out I had made a leadership decision that he didn't like. Instead of coming to me about it, he just built up this silent anger and hostility in his heart such that it didn't matter what I said or did, he was against me. He ultimately did the right thing by coming to me and making things right between us.

God will not bless your life or your leadership if you wear a smile on your face but carry hidden hatred in your heart.

We can learn another lesson from the older brother in the parable of the two sons. He hated his brother. He hated his dad. He hated his responsibilities. He harbored hostility in his heart, kept his mouth shut, and let that hatred build up until it just came pouring out when he did not get his way.

QUESTIONS

Is there anyone you have a hostile attitude towards?

Is there anyone you are against?

Is there anyone who has offended you, hurt you, or done you wrong that you have built up hostility toward?"

ENCOURAGEMENTS

Deal with your hostility.

Talk to God about it.

Ask for His help.

Rehearse the Gospel.

Repent of your sin.

Begin to love that person in a fresh and genuine way.

You can either be a hate-filled liar or a grace-filled ambassador. But you can't be both.

Which one are you going to choose today?

What do you need to do to have a heart of love toward everyone in your life?

_____

_____

_____

▸ DON'T SLANDER ANYONE.

"And whoever utters slander is a fool."

Slander is sharing negative information about a person with the intent to harm that person. It is communicating in such a way that disparages the character and reputation of another person. It's often born out of some wrong that has been done to us or to someone we love. We feel hurt, offended, slighted, or mistreated. So what do we do? We slander that person in order to settle the score, carry out personal revenge, or knock that person down a notch or two.

Slander is revealing. It reveals our selfishness. When someone stands in the way of our agenda, we feel justified to slander. Some years ago, my son did not make the All-Star Team in baseball. From my estimation he was one of the top five or six players in the league. So when the coach told me he didn't make it, my head started spinning and my heart started churning. The temptation to slander the league's coaches was definitely present within my heart. But I knew that whatever I said about them would be rooted in the pain and sting of feeling that my son was unjustly treated. So I tried my best, in the power of the Holy Spirit, to stay calm and move on without harboring any offense or speaking any slanderous words. I don't know why he wasn't selected. No matter what the reason was, legitimate or illegitimate, slandering those coaches would do nothing but build me up, tear them down, and squash any impact that I could have for the kingdom of God.

Slander reveals our unbelief. We lack faith in God's justice. "Vengeance is mine. I will repay," says the Lord. Revenge is not our responsibility. That job belongs to God. When we slander people who hurt or harm us, we are exercising some form of personal revenge.

How can you know if you're slandering someone? You can ask these questions.

- Is what I am saying about this person true or false?

- Am I ascribing motives to the person?

- Am I trying to solve a real problem or air a personal offense?

- Would I be embarrassed if the person heard me say what I just said?

I try to speak in such a way that if everything I ever said about a person got back to that person, I would not be embarrassed, and I could still have a loving relationship with him or her. Now I'll tell you right now, I've not been 100% successful at this through the years, but I have certainly become a more thoughtful and loving friend.

Do some self-evaluation. Do you attack people's character or harm their reputation by the way you talk about them? Do you say things about other players that is mean-spirited? Do you needlessly attack the character of others? Do you air your critical opinions about coaches, players, officials, or administrators to your teammates and friends just because you can? Repent! Resolve to stop slandering people.

Write down some principles you can use when you are being baited or tempted to slander someone.

_____

_____

_____

_____

_____

_____

▶ DON'T BE TALKATIVE. BE TEMPERATE.

"When words are many, transgression is not lacking;

but whoever restrains his lips is prudent."

People who talk all the time invite all kinds of sins into their life – slander, malice, crudeness, rudeness, pride. The Apostle Peter was given to too much talking. That's why he is known as the Apostle with the foot-shaped mouth.

If you're given to talking a lot, then you need to work on restraining your lips. Consciously restrain yourself. Ask more questions. Listen more intently. Draw out the person with whom you're in conversation.

Temperance in communication is a sign of wisdom and love. When I was in seminary, I had some fabulous professors. Not only did I learn from them in class, but I had the privilege to be discipled by them, have lunch with them, and even share dinner with them on occasion. These men "talked" for a living. But they always prayed before each class and asked for God's help in communication. They gave solid instruction and direct answers. In private they were men of choice words. They asked lots of questions and listened intently to our responses. One of my professors, Dr. William Barrick, spoke over ten languages, translated the Bible into Bengali, traveled the world, and had one of the highest IQs of anyone I have ever met. But if I had lunch with him, he asked me as many questions as I asked him. And he genuinely wanted to know the answers.

Listening is a great skill and an act of love. The best relationships and conversations happen when two people want to learn from one another and love one another. No one is trying to prove anything, one-up the other, or get the last word in. No one has any agenda except that God be glorified.

- Do you have a tendency to talk too much?

- Do you have a tendency to go on and on about things?

- Can you use less words to get your point across?

Jesus was not a talker, per se. He was a preacher, a teacher, and a friend. But He was not a talker. Read the Gospels. You never get the impression that He went on and on about things. He used an economy of words, even in His sermons, in order to achieve the greatest effect.

Too many coaches and athletes are "talkers." They just talk and talk and talk. What they don't realize is that the players condition themselves to tune that person out. Every time the person speaks it's like the grown-ups in the cartoon Charlie Brown, "Wah Wah Wa."

List two ways you can become a better communicator and listener:

1. _____

_____

_____

2. _____

_____

_____

▶ HAVE YOUR HEART RIGHT WITH GOD AND YOUR SPEECH RICH WITH PEOPLE.

"The tongue of the righteous is choice silver; the heart of the wicked is of little worth."

In Proverbs the "tongue" is frequently coupled with the "heart." "The heart of the wise makes his speech judicious and adds persuasiveness to his lips" (16:23). "Like the glaze covering an earthen vessel are fervent lips with an evil heart" (26:23). "Whoever hates disguises himself with his lips and harbors deceit in his heart, when he speaks graciously, believe him not, for there are seven abominations in his heart…" (26:24-25).

Your words are a reflection of what's going on inside your heart. The heart of the wicked is of little worth because it beats for self-glory. The heart of the wicked is dark, making his speech untrustworthy. It's not worth very much.

The tongue of the righteous, on the other hand, is choice silver because it comes from the spiritual treasure chest of a redeemed heart. When your life has been radically and eternally changed by God's grace you want every part of your life to be a reflection of that grace, including your speech. "Choice silver" is beautiful, rare, and valuable. So are the words of a righteous person.

Consider the teaching of Jesus in Luke 6:43-45. "For no good tree bears bad fruit, nor again does a bad tree bear good fruit, for each tree is known by its own fruit. For figs are not gathered from thorn bushes, nor are grapes picked from a bramble bush. The good person out of the good treasure of his heart produces good, and the evil person out of his evil treasure produces evil, for out of the abundance of the heart his mouth speaks."

What is the best way to have your heart right with God on a daily basis?

_____

_____

_____

When your peers leave a one-on-one conversation with you, how do you think they feel? How do you want them to feel?

_____

_____

_____

_____

_____

▶ USE YOUR SPEECH TO MEET PEOPLE'S DEEPEST NEEDS.

"The lips of the righteous feed many, but fools die for lack of sense."

The righteous person refreshes and replenishes others with his speech. He feeds others with love, grace, hope, stability, and truth. Fools don't feed others. They take from others and also starve to death due to their lack of connection to the life-giving root of God's love.

There is no "neutral zone" in your speech. You're either building up or tearing down. Your teammates won't remember your big pregame speeches or brilliant words you shared during a time-out. But they will remember how you made them feel day in and day out with your verbal and non-verbal communication. If you are marked by three communication traits, what do you want those traits to be and why?

1. _____

_____

_____

2. _____

_____

_____

3. _____

_____

_____

GAME CHANGER

The officers then came to the chief priests and Pharisees, who said to them, "Why did you not bring him?" The officers answered, "No one ever spoke like this man!"

(John 7:45-46).

No one ever spoke like Jesus. His words were perfect, pure, loving, and powerful. Nothing He ever said was a lie. Everything He ever said was the truth. He spoke no idol or empty words, only meaningful and helpful words. Even when people were hurling the worst of insults at Him while He hung on the cross, He spoke words of forgiveness and love, "Father, forgive them for they know not what they do."

Jesus changes the game when it comes to our speech. First of all, His perfect record of righteous speech before God becomes our record before God. Second, the Spirit who enabled Him to speak lovingly every day resides inside of us and guides us, as well. Third, He has left us an account of His speech in the Gospels so that we can learn from Him and be more like Him in our communication.

He saves us in His redemptive work. He strengthens us in the giving of His Spirit. He sets the standard for us by His own example.

ONE BIG THING

What is the most significant lesson for you to take with you from this chapter?

_____

_____

_____

_____

_____

_____

_____

_____

IMPACT PRAYER

Father in heaven, thank You for sending people to communicate the words of life to us. Please help us to be athletes who speak the words of life to our family, peers, and teammates. In the name of Jesus, Amen.

★ ★ ★

CHAPTER SIX

DISCERNING ATHLETES

WALK HUMBLY

PROVERBS 11:2

STUDY STARTER

I grew up with a kid who was a good athlete and a really good pitcher. He had a good fast ball, a wicked curve ball, and an effective change-up. From the time we were in Little League he made it his mission to inform me about how good he was.

- "Did you hear about my no-hitter?"
- "I struck out 13 batters last Friday night."
- "My ERA is 1.15."
- "I haven't allowed an extra base-hit in six starts."
- "I have 7 scholarship offers."

When we were real young, I just listened to him. But then I realized that he probably needed someone to help him understand that his boasting wasn't all that winsome. So I started playing along with him and would say things like, "Dude, you're incredible! I mean, you could become the greatest pitcher of all time. You could have the fast-ball of Nolan Ryan and the curve ball of Sandy Koufax. We could call you Nolan Koufax." I thought this tactic may dissuade him. It didn't.

Few of us are so blatant and bold with our boasts. No, our pride is more subtle than that, much more subliminal, and much more devious. When we think of pride, we inevitably think of that person who brags all the time, talks about himself, and wants everyone to notice him. When we think of pride, certain people come to our minds. But none of us thinks first of ourselves. You see, pride is blinding. We can spot it a mile away in someone else, but we can't see it in ourselves if we're looking at a mirror twelve inches from our face.

The goal of this chapter is to reveal the ugliness of pride and the beauty of humility, to convince you that a life of humility is better and sweeter than a life of pride, and to help you cultivate a culture of humility on your teams. Let's look to Proverbs 11:2 to help us do that.

STUDY PASSAGE

² When pride comes, then comes disgrace,

but with the humble is wisdom.

STUDY HELP

"pride" = Literally, to boil over the edge of the pot. Spiritually, to be full of yourself, to allow your heart and mind to fixate on your desires, your agenda, your plans, your success, your failure, your family, your job, your hobbies. If you are prideful, then you are the center of the universe. Everything rotates around you. In your mind and heart, everyone exists to serve you, love you, and exalt you. You know more than everyone else. You're better than everyone else. You're wiser than everyone else. You're more skilled than everyone else. For that reason, you don't listen to advice or receive instruction. You are full of yourself.

"comes" = enters.

"disgrace" = shame, dishonor. It doesn't say how or when the disgrace will come, it just says that it will. But it comes because you are full of yourself and empty of wisdom. You are so intoxicated with yourself and rebellious toward God that you do your own thing, in your own way, in spite of His glory and wisdom. Ultimately, the folly of your self-centeredness catches up with you and you are disgraced.

There are many biblical examples of pride leading to disgrace. Here are but a few.

- In Genesis 11:5-8 the people of Babel said, "Let us make a name for ourselves..." That didn't end well for them.

- In Numbers 12:2 Aaron and Miriam asked, "What about us?!" Miriam became leprous.

- In 2 Chronicles 26:16-21 King Uzziah's pride led to the shame of leprosy.

- In Esther 5:11 and 7:10 Haman's pride led to his death.

- In Luke 18:9-14 the self-righteous Pharisee's pride led to eternal shame.

"humble" = modest, levelheaded. If you are humble, you see God for who He really is and yourself for who you really are. You see yourself as God sees you. You embrace your identity and calling through the lens of Scripture. You understand that there is a God, and you are not Him. You embrace the fact that you a fallen person created and sustained by a good God. He doesn't exist for your glory. You exist for His glory. You embrace the fact that life is best when God is in the center of your heart and mind.

"wisdom" = the skill of effectively navigating all of life toward the glory of God.

There are also many biblical examples of humility leading to wisdom.

- Mordecai and Esther humbled themselves before the Lord. He gave them wisdom to know how to save the Israelite people.

- Nehemiah was distraught over the ruin of Jerusalem and the peril of his people. He humbled himself before the Lord and gained the wisdom to successfully appeal to the King.

- Naomi and Ruth were in dire straits. They humbled themselves together before the Lord and He gave them wisdom to handle their difficult circumstances.

- The Syrophoenician mother was desperate for her ailing daughter to be healed. Consider the depth of her humility in this account. **Immediately a woman whose little daughter had an unclean spirit heard of him and came and fell down at his feet. Now the woman was a Gentile, a Syrophoenician by birth. And she begged him to cast the demon out of her daughter. And he said to her, "Let the children be fed first, for it is not right to take the children's bread and throw it to the dogs." But she answered him, "Yes, Lord; yet even the dogs under the table eat the children's crumbs." And he said to her, "For this statement you may go your way; the demon has left your daughter." And she went home and found the child lying in bed and the demon gone (Mark 7:25-30).** This woman's humility gave her the wisdom to speak with Jesus in a faith-filled manner. He rewarded her spirit of lowliness.

Consider the paradox of Proverbs 11:2. When you're full of yourself, you'll be made empty of honor. But when you're empty of yourself, you'll be made full of wisdom. If you make yourself high, you'll be made low. If you make yourself low, you'll be made high. It sounds a lot like the teaching of Jesus: "For whoever would save his life will lose it, but whoever loses his life for my sake will save it." (Luke 9:24)

Scripture teaches so many principles about pride and humility.

- God opposes the proud but gives grace to the humble. (James 4:6)

- Everyone who is arrogant in heart is an abomination to the Lord; be assured, he will not go unpunished. (Proverbs 16:5)

- What does the Lord require of you but to do justice, and to love kindness, and to walk humbly with your God? (Micah 6:8)

STUDY QUESTIONS

1. What is the result of pride?

_____

_____

_____

_____

2. What is the result of humility?

_____

_____

_____

_____

3. According to what you know about Scripture and the plight of humanity, why are people plagued with personal pride?

_____

_____

_____

_____

4. Give an example of how a posture of humility can lead a person to a life of wisdom.

_____

_____

_____

_____

5. Even though Jesus is the eternal Son of God worthy of universal praise and worship, He is humble. Describe in detail how Jesus has exemplified humility. Consider these passages: Matthew 27:27-44 and Hebrews 12:1-2

_____

_____

_____

6. Do you know an athlete who is very successful and very humble at the same time? How do you think he or she maintains humility while achieving great success?

_____

_____

_____

_____

STUDY SUMMARY

The self-consumed life of pride leads to disgrace, but the self-giving life of humility leads to wisdom.

ATHLETE CONNECTION

As a discerning athlete, you will embrace a life of humility for yourself and integrate it into the culture of your team. You will impact your teammates by showing that the way up is down and the way high is low.

KEYS TO WINNING

▶ VIDEO GUIDE AT KINGDOMSPORTS.ONLINE

▶ RUN FROM PRIDE.

Pride pursues personal glory instead of God's glory. Pride is the personal commitment to steal glory from God and achieve glory for yourself. It is to be so full of yourself that you have no room for God and others. The only reason a prideful person would find room for God and others is if that would somehow help him achieve his highest goal of personal glory. And that does happen. Being seen as religious or service-oriented is a way some people feed their ego. Pride is the attempt to glorify self, promote self, satisfy self, and serve self at the expense of God's glory and others' happiness.

Pride is natural. It is rooted in our innate human desire for glory. We were made for glory. But in our fallenness, God's glory is not our natural aim. Personal glory is! Pride is our default setting.

Pride steals from God what belongs to Him and parades it around as if nothing is wrong or out of order. When I was in the ninth grade one of my classmates reached into my PE locker and stole my new Nike wind pants. He didn't go sell them. He didn't give them to his brother. He didn't wait awhile to wear them. No. The very next day he marched on to campus wearing those pants. There was no shame in his game. He was bold! So is pride. When we pursue our own glory, we take from God what rightfully belongs to Him and wear it around as if it belongs to us.

Pride motivates you to commit all kinds of other sins.

- **Argumentativeness** is rooted in pride. You argue with another player because you want to prove to him that you're right. You want to be right because you're committed to promote yourself and glorify yourself.

- **Laziness** is rooted in pride. You don't complete your taxes on time because you don't feel like it. You are more committed to satisfy your desire to watch ballgames than serving the needs of your family.

- **Self-promotion** is rooted in pride. You brag about your accomplishments because you want your buddies to know how good of a player you are.

- **Unwillingness** to serve is rooted in pride. You don't sign up for service opportunities at your church because you don't want that kind of commitment. You don't want that kind of commitment because it doesn't promote your agenda or satisfy your desire to be served.

- **Slander** is rooted in pride. You say some bad things about a teammate to your coach. You accuse him of being lazy. Why? Because you know that the starting position will down to you or him. So you try to get an advantage over him in the coach's eyes. Why? Because you are committed to promote yourself at the expense of others.

- **Anger** is rooted in pride. You demand to have things your way. If you don't get your way, then everyone in your family or on your team is going to know about it and feel your wrath. That's pride.

- **Materialism** is rooted in pride. You demand the best shoes, the nicest car, and the finest clothes. You believe you deserve these things. And your commitment to personal glory demands these things.

Pride enslaves you to your personal agenda. It binds you to the agenda of the unholy trinity of Me, Myself, and I. If you can't get some kind of glory, some measure of comfort, some kind of physical satisfaction or material gain from it, then you won't do it. If you are prideful, then you are enslaved to the ball-and-chain of personal glory. That is a very restrictive place to be.

Have you ever looked at another Christian who consistently loves God and serves others with joy and asked yourself the question, "How does he do that?" The answer to that question is easy: he has been set free from the prison-house of pride. He has been liberated from the slavery of self-promotion. He has tasted the fresh water of humility and found it to be more satisfying and more glorious than the agenda of self-glory. The world's smallest package is a man wrapped up in himself. But the world's greatest gift is a person who is fully committed to pursue the glory of God and the joy of others.

No one is immune to pride. Though it shows up in different forms and in different degrees, it infects every one of us. The real issue is not if pride exists in your heart, but where it exists and how you can rid yourself of it.

In what areas of your life are you still holding tight to your glory and agenda? Take some time to honestly answer the following questions.

Are you willing to be corrected or unwilling to be corrected?

_____

Give a recent example of when you were wrong and willingly received correction from another person:

_____

_____

Are you respectful of authority or dismissive of authority?

_____

Give a recent example of how you honored your authority's wishes when you would have preferred to do it another way.

_____

_____

Are you generally condescending or encouraging to people?

_____

Give an example of how you intentionally encourage people on a daily basis.

_____

_____

Do you routinely run away from or toward sacrificial service to others?

_____

Give a recent example of how you volunteered to serve someone that had nothing to do with your own agenda to gain something.

_____

_____

Do you exercise compassion or lack compassion for people in need?

_____

Give a recent example of how you exercised compassion on a friend, teammate, coach, family member, or stranger who needed to feel love of God.

_____

_____

Do you regularly or rarely ask people for forgiveness?

_____

When is the last time you confessed your sin against someone and asked them to forgive you?

_____

_____

Do you get happy or jealous when your peers succeed?

_____

When is the last time you rejoiced over the success of another person?

How did you express that joy?

_____

_____

Pride is something that God hates and condemns. Proverbs 16:5 is explicit about this, *"Everyone who is proud in heart is an abomination to the Lord; assuredly he will not go unpunished." So run from it. Run as far away from it as you can.*

▶ RUN TO HUMILITY.

Humility pursues God's glory and others' joy. Humility starts by seeing yourself for who you really are, by seeing yourself as God sees you. Humility is a mindset, but it is more than a mindset. It's a way of life. It's a life of worship and service. Humility is the personal commitment to glorify God and serve others because Jesus Christ has served and saved you.

Humility is not marked by self-pity, but self-forgetfulness. Humility is not thinking terrible things about yourself. It's not staring in the mirror and saying, "I'm such a bad person. I'm worthless. I'm nothing." No! Humility is simply not staring in the mirror. It's finding your joy in the glory of God and the joy of others.

We have an innate and unhealthy fascination with ourselves. So even when we grasp the concept that we're not supposed to be consumed with our glory, we can wrongly over-compensate for that and think that we're supposed to be consumed with our failures and shortcomings. That's just as wrong and just as prideful.

What does humility do for you? It liberates you to joyfully pursue God's agenda. Pride is bondage. But humility is freedom. It's liberation. If you're humble, you are unconcerned with personal glory. You're not trying everything you can to get what you want! Humility is liberating because you're not concerned about getting. You're concerned about giving. And you don't need other people's approval, admiration, or adoration to give. Humility is liberating because you can be who God has called you to be and do what God has called you to do with no concern for the praise of man.

These are some great benefits to humility.

- You're not anxious about getting a fair deal.

- You're not worried about receiving praise.

- You're not so self-consumed that you feel the need to put others down when you feel threatened by their skill or expertise.

- You're not jealous when someone else succeeds.

- You're not angry when you don't get your way. As a matter of fact, you're not zealous for your way. You zealous for God's way.

This is why humility leads to wisdom. When you remove the obstacle of self-glory from your heart, then you will have an amazing skill to navigate your life toward the glory of God. Why? Because nothing stands between your agenda and God's agenda. Your agenda is God's agenda.

Principle: The self-consumed life of pride leads to disgrace, but the self-giving life of humility leads to wisdom.

Consider how humility motivates you to worship God and serve people in all kinds of beautiful ways.

- You trust God, rather than blame God.

- You love God, rather than despise God.

- You pray to God, rather than ignore God.

- You thank God for what you have, rather than complain about you don't have.

- You see yourself as equal to others, not better than others.

- You express thankfulness for other people, instead of ignoring their contribution to your welfare.

- You listen intently to others, rather than talking incessantly.

- You build others up, rather than tear them down.

- You have a teachable and correctable spirit.

- You serve voluntarily and sacrificially.

- You confess your sin and repent quickly.

- You grant forgiveness quickly.

- You do your best to overlook other people's mistakes.

- You love and serve people with no expectation to be loved back in the same way.

Todd Blackledge, former NFL quarterback and current football commentator, has said this about humility, "Discipline and diligence are up there on the list, but one of the most important qualities of many really successful people is humility. If you have a degree of humility about you, you have the ability to take advice, to be coachable, teachable. A humble person never stops learning."

Tony Bennett, a championship winning college basketball coach, has made humility the first of five pillars in his basketball program. "Humility is not thinking too highly of yourself. It's not thinking too lowly of yourself. It's knowing who you are as a person and player. It's not thinking less of yourself, but thinking of yourself less… The most humbling thing to me personally is remembering who I was before I had a relationship with Christ and who I am now that I have a relationship with Him. That is the most powerful aspect of humility for me personally."

Tony Bennett has made humility the first pillar of his program. He talks about it. He teaches it. He models it. How can you develop genuine humility in your own life and spread it to others?

_____

_____

_____

_____

_____

_____

GAME CHANGER

Read Philippians 2:1-11 and be in awe of how Jesus is the ultimate Game Changer when it comes to a living a life of humility. Look at Him. Be in awe of Him. Learn from Him.

1 So if there is any encouragement in Christ, any comfort from love, any participation in the Spirit, any affection and sympathy,

2 complete my joy by being of the same mind, having the same love, being in full accord and of one mind.

3 Do nothing from selfish ambition or conceit, but in humility count others more significant than yourselves.

4 Let each of you look not only to his own interests, but also to the interests of others.

5 Have this mind among yourselves, which is yours in Christ Jesus,

6 Who, though He was in the form of God, did not count equality with God a thing to be grasped,

7 but emptied Himself, by taking the form of a servant, being born in the likeness of men.

8 And being found in human form, He humbled Himself, by becoming obedient to the point of death, even death on a cross.

9 Therefore God has highly exalted Him and bestowed on Him the name that is above every name,

10 so that at the name of Jesus every knee should bow, in heaven and on earth and under the earth

11 and every tongue confess that Jesus Christ is Lord, to the glory of God the Father.

ONE BIG THING

What is the most significant lesson for you to take with you from this chapter?

_____

_____

_____

_____

_____

_____

_____

IMPACT PRAYER

Father in heaven, You are so gracious to show us the perils of pride and blessings of humility. Without that illumination we would spend our lives pursuing selfish goals that have no eternal worth. Thank You. And thank You for the humble example of the Lord Jesus. Please help us to follow in His footsteps of humility for the glory of Your name and the good of those we lead. In the name of Jesus we pray, Amen.

* * *

CHAPTER SEVEN

DISCERNING ATHLETES

BLESS THEIR CITIES

PROVERBS 11:10-11

STUDY STARTER

You are a leader. God calls leaders to leverage their skills for the good of people in their circle of influence. You have an expanding circle of influence. It starts with your family. It runs to your closest friends. Then it increases to teammates, coaches, competitors, and fans. Ultimately it expands to the city in which you live and compete.

You have three basic options when it comes to how you relate to your city:

- You can be a burden, a person who weighs down the city with your attitude, actions, and influence.
- You can be a bystander, a person who watches the city with your attitude, actions, and influence.
- You can be a blessing, a person who blesses the city with your attitude, actions, and influence.

The proverb you're about to study will encourage and challenge you to be intentional about using your leadership to bless your city.

STUDY PASSAGE

[10] When it goes well with the righteous, the city rejoices
and when the wicked perish there are shouts of gladness.
[11] By the blessing of the upright a city is exalted,
but by the mouth of the wicked it is overthrown.

STUDY HELP

Reading different Bible versions of this proverb will be helpful to grasp its meaning and importance. The bold phrases are supplied by me so that you'll see the results of good leaders upon their communities.

Easy-to-Read Version (ERV)

- When good people are successful, **the whole city is happy**,
- and they all shout for joy when evil people are destroyed.
- Blessings from the honest people living in a city **will make it great**,
- but the things evil people say can destroy it.

Expanded Bible (EXB)

- When good people succeed, **the city is happy**.
- When evil people die, there are shouts of joy.
- Good people **bless and build up their city**,
- but the wicked can destroy it with their words.

The Living Bible (TLB)

- **The whole city celebrates** a good man's success –
- and also the godless man's death.
- **The good influence of godly citizens causes a city to prosper**,
- but the moral decay of the wicked drives it downhill.

The Voice

- When prosperity comes to those who do right, **the whole city celebrates**;
- but when the wicked get their just punishment, there is joyous cheering.
- **A city thrives through the blessing of those living right**,
- but the words of a wrongdoer will bring it to ruin.

ESV

- When it goes well with the righteous, **the city rejoices**
- and when the wicked perish there are shouts of gladness.
- By the blessing of the upright **a city is exalted**,
- but by the mouth of the wicked it is overthrown.

But what is a city? In Old Testament culture, the city was the centerpiece of population, commerce, and socialization. The thing that distinguished a city from a town or village was whether or not it had walls for defense. A city was known as the mother and its surrounding villages were known as its daughters. As a matter of fact, the original Hebrew word for village literally means daughter. But something important about the word "city" here in Proverbs 11:10-11 is that it can mean "city, village, or town." It's not trying to paint a picture of a big place with tall walls or a small place with no walls. It's simply trying to paint a picture of where you live! **So a city is the place you live and the people you see.**

STUDY QUESTIONS

1. What does the city do when righteous people succeed?

_____

_____

_____

2. What does the city do when evil people perish?

_____

_____

_____

3. What happens to a city when righteous people bless it?

_____

_____

_____

4. What happens to a city when righteous people do nothing, and wicked people insert themselves into places of influence?

_____

_____

_____

_____

5. Have you ever personally experienced the prosperity of a city, where people were blessed, safe, successful? Describe that environment and the people who helped make it that way.

_____

_____

_____

_____

6. Have you ever personally experienced the downfall of a city, where people were downtrodden, in danger, and struggling to make it? Describe that environment and the kind of people who contributed to that downturn.

_____

_____

_____

_____

_____

STUDY SUMMARY

Be a blessing to your city by being a righteous person.

ATHLETE CONNECTION

As a discerning athlete you will leverage your life and leadership to bless your city.

KEYS TO WINNING

▶ **VIDEO GUIDE AT KINGDOMSPORTS.ONLINE**

▶ BE RIGHTEOUS.

What is a righteous person? First, let me tell you what he is not.

A righteous person is **not self-righteous.** He doesn't believe that he possesses moral superiority. He doesn't pride himself in being "better" than others. He doesn't look at other worshipers and judge them as inferior to himself. He doesn't look at unbelievers and feel that he is a cut above. He doesn't pray what the Pharisee prayed in Luke 18:9-14, "God, I thank you that I am not like other men, extortioners, unjust, adulterers, or even like this tax collector."

A righteous person is **not self-consumed.** There is a brand of Christianity that is inwardly focused to a fault. It is consumed with "*my* Bible reading, *my* Bible knowledge, *my* prayer life, *my* family worship time, *my* Sunday morning worship service, *my* Wednesday night Bible studies, *my* men's small group, *my* accountability partner." It looks really religious and righteous. People hear about all the religious things he is doing and say, "Man, that guy must be godly!" But in reality, he has turned his Christianity into a house of mirrors. That's not righteous. *Any form of Christianity that doesn't regularly involve sacrificial love for people who need Jesus is not the Christianity that Jesus established.* True righteousness is not consumed with self.

A righteous person is **not unrestrained or licentious**. There are Christians who take great pride in the excesses of their lives. I know of church music leaders who drink alcohol and smoke marijuana in the parking lot prior to their worship music practice. I know of a music leader who was asked to play background music from his iTunes list. He quickly replied, "Dude there's no music in my phone that would be appropriate for a worship setting." Once I was invited to play ball at an area high school on the weekend by some church leaders. They brought beer to the campus. I was thinking in my mind, "What galaxy are these guys from? Apparently, the galaxy that pays no attention to the regulations of the local school board." Listen, righteous people have freedom. But they don't flaunt their freedom around as if their liberty is the most important thing in the world to them. *Righteous people are chiefly concerned with demonstrating the righteous character of God and considering the weaknesses of others.*

A righteous person is **not a legalist.** A legalist is a person who lives by the rules and tries to earn his salvation by rule-keeping. A legalist says, "Just give me the rules sheet. Just tell me what I can do and can't do, and I'll take it from there." Legalism seeks to gain the favor of God by performing for Him. A legalist's joy rises and falls on how excellently he is keeping the rules. A legalist is typically arrogant, unloving toward people who aren't just like himself, and unwilling to help other Christians who don't abide by the same rules and regulations that he does. The righteous man is not a legalist. The righteous man knows he has broken the rules. He is very aware that he has fallen short of God's righteous standards. Not only has he broken the rules in the past, but he will do so again in the future. He doesn't trust in his own righteousness, but in the righteousness of Jesus Christ.

If he is not self-righteous, self-consumed, unrestrained, or a legalist, then what is he? A righteous person is one who lives in awe of God, pursues the character of God, and expresses the love of God.

A righteous person **lives in awe of God.** Awe is wonder, thrill, and reverence wrapped up in one. When we gaze at the magnificent beauty and excellence of our God, we can't help but be in awe of Him. I remember the first time I visited Yosemite National Park. As I entered the park I drove through a large tunnel and came out the other side. What I saw next was nothing short of majestic. It was sheer beauty. The valley, mountains, trees, waterfalls, cliffs, rocks, birds, and streams dazzled my eyes. It was more than I could absorb in one moment. I was in awe. God is like that, only better. He is loving, gracious, holy, mighty, sovereign, just, merciful, compassionate, loyal, forgiving, faithful, and good all at the same time. Everything that is good in your life is because of Him. Every awesome thing that you see with your eyes, smell with your nose, feel with your hands, taste with your mouth, and hear with your ears is from Him and designed to point you to Him. The righteous person understands that and daily lives in awe of God.

A righteous person **pursues the character of God.** Because God is righteous, the righteous person wants to be like Him. The righteous person wants to lie less and tell the truth more. He wants to be less lazy and more diligent. He wants to run from pride and run to humility. He wants to hold less grudges and freely forgive more people. He wants to be less selfish and more selfless. He wants to be less stingy and more generous. He wants all those things and more because he knows that those things reflect the character of the God who has loved, forgiven, and redeemed him. The righteous person actively pursues the character of God.

A righteous person **expresses the love of God.** The modern strategy of how to live life is to "get all you can, can all you get, sit on the lid, and let no one have anything that you've put inside." People label that philosophy with many tags – frugality, efficiency, conservative, tight, etc. But the righteous person understands and embraces the fact that to whom much has been given, much is required. The righteous person has been a recipient of the amazing grace of almighty God. When God changed the righteous person's life it was as if God backed a massive dump truck up to the person's heart and unloaded tons of mercy, grace, love, forgiveness, and freedom at the same time. Because of that, the righteous person is so overwhelmed with God's love that he can't help but share that love with the people around him. He can't hold it in. He can't store it away. It's too good. He has to give it to the people around him so they can experience the same love that he has. He grieves for the people who live in bitterness, hopelessness, selfishness, and depression. So he makes it his mission to love others the way God has loved him.

Look back at what a righteous person is not and what a righteous person is. On the negative side, consider which one of those "not" traits you need to work on the most. Write down how you plan to do that. Then consider which one of those positive traits you would like to improve on the most and how you'd like to do that.

A righteous person is not…

A righteous person is…

▶ EMBRACE YOUR CITY.

The fate of the city is important, because the city is made up of people. And people matter to God. People are created in the image of God for enjoyment with God to the glory of God. The city matters because people matter.

So when you think "city" don't first think of the city taxes, city budget, city hall, city infrastructure, city development, city schools, city parks, or city water. All that stuff contributes to the function of the city to be sure. But when you first think of the city you should think of the children who get on the school bus at 6:15am and go eat their free breakfast in the cafeteria. Think of the 82-year-old widow who lives in a nursing home around the corner. Think of the 40-year-old single mom who manages the McDonald's by your practice field. Think of the hair stylist at Sport Clips; the single dad who works second shift at a manufacturing plant; the immigrant family who lives in the mobile home park by the airport; the couple who owns and operates the gas station you frequent; and all the boys and girls who play rec league sports at the local YMCA.

These are happy people and sad people. These are good people and bad people. These are people who have their act together and people whose lives are tearing apart at the seams. They are people who love God and people who have no idea who the real God is and how much He longs for them to know the joy of worshiping Him.

The city is the people. And they aren't hypothetical, faceless people. They are people just like us. They have real lives, real dreams, real desires, real problems, and real fears. And what they need is real people who know the real God to bring real love, listening, and wisdom to them so they can know and experience the fullness of God's blessing.

Consider your circle of influence in the city. Take some time to write down a few names of people in each of the concentric circles of your city. Then pray, asking God to give you conviction to embrace each of them with God's love.

Family Members:

_____

_____

Neighbors:

_____

_____

Teammates:

_____

_____

Coaches:

_____

_____

Friends:

_____

_____

People at Church:

_____

_____

Teachers/Administrators:

_____

_____

Mayor/City Councilpersons:

_____

_____

First Responders (Fire, Police, EMT):

_____

_____

Business people:

_____

_____

Miscellaneous people:

_____

_____

▶PLAN YOUR WORK AND WORK YOUR PLAN.

You've heard that the road to hell is paved with good intentions. I tell you that the path to a cursed and condemned city is paved with lots of good, general intentions to bless people and no specific resolution to carry it out day to day, month to month, year to year.

Start blessing your city by blessing those in your concentric circles. Ask these questions:

How can I personally be a consistent blessing to those people?

_____

_____

How can my family be a consistent blessing to our city?

_____

_____

How can my team be a consistent blessing to our city?

_____

_____

When I was a kid Rocky Riddle moved to my city and became the youth sports director for Childersburg, Alabama. He immediately initiated a youth soccer league for the first time ever. No one in Childersburg had played soccer. He created a weekly youth event called Friday Night Live. We played games, listened to inspirational messages, and set the world record for the longest banana split (or so we thought). He established a youth leadership team that met in his house and planned events for other kids. His presence and love for our city was felt in a significant way. He blessed us with his energy, creativity, and love. I remember scoring three goals in a soccer game and Rocky later presented me with a hat. I asked him, "What is this for?" He said, "If you score three goals, it's called a hat trick. Here is your hat. You earned it." I thought that was the best thing ever! I wore that hat with honor.

Cities need people like that. And as an athlete you have the great privilege to bring that kind of energy, hope, and love to people in your city. Would you spend a few minutes considering a sustained way in which you can love your city and rally other athletes and coaches to join you in the effort?

_____

_____

_____

_____

_____

_____

GAME CHANGER

Jesus was a blessing to His city. He preached the Gospel to the city. He cared for the struggling members of the city (e.g., He healed Peter's mother-in-law). He prayed for the city. He stood against the self-righteous leaders of the city. He invested His life into the men of the city. He offered hope to the scariest people in the city (e.g., Mark 5:1-20). He fed hungry people in the city. He counseled people in the city (e.g., Nicodemus, the Rich Young Ruler). He spent time with people in the city ("He dined with tax collectors and sinners."). He respected the authority of the city ("Render to Caesar what belongs to Caesar"). He endured the sins of the city. He died for the sins of the city. He rose for the life of the city.

Jesus was truly righteous. He embraced His city. He planned His work and worked His plan. As a result, redemption is available to all who believe in Him.

When it comes to blessing your city as a discerning athlete, first look to Jesus as your Redeemer and Lord, then as your Leader and Example.

ONE BIG THING

What is the most significant lesson for you to take with you from this chapter?

_____

_____

_____

_____

_____

_____

_____

IMPACT PRAYER

Father in heaven, You came to us in the cities in which we lived through our parents, teachers, coaches, preachers, and neighbors. And You shaped and changed us through them. Please help us do the same for others in our cities. Help us to be a blessing. For the glory of Jesus. Amen.

★ ★ ★

CHAPTER EIGHT
DISCERNING ATHLETES
MODEL FRIENDSHIP

PROVERBS 17:17

STUDY STARTER

Sovereign Grace Music struck spiritual gold with their song on friendship. It is titled "A Good Friend."

Verse 1

A friend will always think of others

A friend will overlook a wrong

A friend sticks closer than a brother

A friend is patient all along

Jesus, let me be the friend You are to me

Verse 2

A friend will help me do the right things

A friend won't lead me into sin

A friend will help me when I stumble

A friend will lift me up again

Jesus, help me find a friend who'll make me wise

Chorus

A good friend, true friend

Here to help you through friend

Strong friend, kind friend

You can have what's mine, friend

Best friend, sure friend

Humble and a pure friend

Lord, I wanna be a good friend

That song embodies what Proverbs teaches about friendship. You are made for friendship. And so are your teammates. We are all made to be in relationships of mutual love, laughter, sacrifice, and blessing. As we meditate on Proverbs 17:17, let's trust the Holy Spirit to help us have closer friendships with others and sweeter friendship with the Lord.

STUDY PASSAGE

¹⁷ A friend loves at all times,

and a brother is born for adversity.

STUDY HELP

We have an interpretation opportunity with this proverb. The first phrase is straightforward. But the second needs consideration. There are two options as to what the phrase "and a brother is born for adversity" actually means. Let's consider the two options and arrive at a conclusion based on sound bible study principles.

Interpretive Option 1: "A true friend loves consistently at all times, but a brother (a sibling) is born to love during the hardest times." Let me personalize this option for even greater clarity. "Ben Brown is my friend. He loves me all the time. He loves me in the routine flow of everyday life. But Scott Limbaugh is my brother. He was born to love me when I'm at my lowest, weakest point in life. When I'm really struggling with a major problem, I should call him because he was born for this kind of thing."

Interpretive Option 2: "A friend loves consistently at all times; yes a brother (a true friend) is born to courageously love at the most difficult times." Again, I will personalize it for clarity. "Ben Brown is my friend. He consistently loves me at all times. Yes, he is a true spiritual brother. He courageously loves me when I'm going through the most difficult of circumstances. He is a true friend, a beloved brother."

Biblically, we can make a case for both interpretations:

- Argument for Option 1: The book of Proverbs has two other passages that distinguish "**friend**" from "**brother**." And the Apostle Paul teaches that family members should take care of one another. Proverbs 18:24 says, "A man of many companions may come to ruin, but there is a friend who sticks closer than a brother." Proverbs 27:10 says, "Do not forsake your friend or your father's friend, and do not go to your brother's house in the day of your calamity. Better is a neighbor who is near than a brother who is far away." 1 Timothy 5:8 says, "If anyone does not provide for his relatives, and especially members of his household, he has denied the faith and is worse than an unbeliever."

- Argument for Option 2: The Bible teaches that a true friend is a spiritual "brother." David said in 2 Samuel 1:26, "I am distressed for you, **my brother Jonathan**; very pleasant have you been to me; your love to me was extraordinary, surpassing the love of women." Jesus said in Mark 3:31-35, "Who are my mother and my brothers?

110

…Here are my mother and my brothers! For **whoever does the will of God, he is my brother** and sister and mother." Paul said in Romans 12:5, 10, "We…are one body in Christ…and individually members one of another… **Love one another with brotherly affection.**." In his letter to the Thessalonians Paul called his spiritual friends **"brothers"** three times.

Additional factors bolster the likelihood of both options. But after careful consideration and prayer my interpretation is Option 2. This is why. The phrase "**at all times**" is the very first phrase in the Hebrew verse. "**At all times**" has primary emphasis. The proverb is clearly focusing on the faithfulness, permanence, and sacrifice of true friendship, true brotherly love.

- The basic idea, then, is this: "**At all times, in all seasons of life, a true friend consistently loves you and pursues your highest good. Yes, in the most troubling and traumatic times of your life a true brother (i.e., a true friend) rises to the occasion to courageously serve you and meet your deepest needs.**"

STUDY QUESTIONS

1. How often does a friend love?

_____

_____

_____

2. Consider the phrase "at all times." List five different "times" a friend should love.

1)_____

2)_____

3)_____

4)_____

5)_____

3. Why is a brother born?

_____

_____

_____

4. Adversity is a time of distress, anxiety, crisis, or need. List five adversities (big or small) you have experienced in life.

1)_____

2)_____

3)_____

4)_____

5)_____

5. List three ways your friends met you in your adversity and blessed you there.

1)_____

_____

2)_____

_____

3)_____

_____

6. God created friendship. He wants us to experience and enjoy friendship. Based on what you know about God's priorities and purposes, what do you think it means to be a true friend?

_____

_____

_____

_____

_____

STUDY SUMMARY

You were made for friendships. To be a true friend you must be consistent in your love and courageous in your service.

ATHLETE CONNECTION

As a discerning athlete you will model what it means to be a great friend by being a great teammate. They need to see and feel how teammates should treat each other. And you can show them the way.

KEYS TO WINNING

▶ **VIDEO GUIDE AT KINGDOMSPORTS.ONLINE**

▶ BE CONSISTENT IN YOUR LOVE.

The first thing you have to do to be a friend is to understand friendship. You can't be a friend if you don't know what friendship is.

A true friend is a trustworthy companion who consistently and lovingly seeks your highest good for the glory of God.

Let's break that definition down.

Trustworthy – a friend can be trusted. He is reliable. If he says he's going to do something, he does it. If you've confided in him with some secret, he doesn't go yell it from the rooftops.

Companion – is a person who is frequently in the company of or associates with another. A companion is someone who does life with you. Even if you are separated by a long distance, you find a way to stay in touch and have meaningful correspondence.

Consistently – There are lots of people who come in and out of our lives, kind of like the UPS guy. We love the UPS guy, don't we? Every time we see him, he makes us happy and brings a smile to our faces because he is bringing us something we ordered. But the UPS guy is not our friend. Number 1, we don't really know him that well. Number 2, we never know when he is going to show up next. A friend, on the other hand, is consistent in his love, his presence, his encouragement. If you have a true friend you don't spend weeks, months, or years waiting to see if he is going to call or text or visit. Why? Because he is consistent.

Lovingly – I used the word lovingly to capture a lot of different concepts. What I mean by lovingly is this: enthusiastically, patiently, sacrificially, generously.

Seeks your highest good – First, he seeks. A true friend is not passive. He doesn't sit around waiting to be loved, cared for, or coddled. He is not in this friendship to soak but to serve. So he actively pursues this friendship. Second, he seeks his friend's highest good. A friend wants joy and success for the other person and will try his best to contribute to that.

For the glory of God – a true friend has the honor and praise of God Himself as his chief motivation for being your friend. Does he want to enjoy laughter? Yes. Does he want to have someone to simply rest and relax with? Absolutely. Does he desire encouragement and help in time of need? Of course. But at the end of the day, his goal for your friendship is that the beauty of God's love and excellence of God's character will be experienced in your life and in his. A true friend wants God to be magnified in your life.

That's why J.C. Ryle made the following comments about choosing friends: "Never make an intimate friend of anyone who is not a friend of God… I do not mean that you ought to have nothing to do with any but true Christians. To take such a line is neither possible nor desirable in this world. Christianity requires no man to be uncourteous. But I advise you to be very careful in your choice of friends… Never be satisfied with the friendship of anyone who will not be useful to your soul… Do you ask me what kinds of friends you shall choose? Choose friends who will benefit your soul – friends whom you can really respect – friends whom you would like to have near you on your deathbed – friends who love the Bible, and are not afraid to speak to you about it – friends such as you will not be ashamed of owning at the coming of Christ, and the day of judgment."

So a true friend is a trustworthy companion who consistently and lovingly seeks your highest good for the glory of God.

Can you think of some relationships you have seen in the Bible that fit the friendship criteria of the definition above? Consider friendships in books like Ruth, First and Second Samuel, and Acts. Write a couple friendships down and describe how their friendship was demonstrated. If you don't know much about friends in the Bible, do a little research on David and Jonathan, Ruth and Naomi, or Paul and Barnabas:

1. _____

_____

_____

2. _____

_____

_____

The second thing you must do to be consistent in your love is understand the consistent love of your ultimate friend and elder brother, Jesus Christ. Hebrews 2:11 teaches us that Jesus is not ashamed to call us his "brothers."

Consider the Lord's words in John 15:12, "This is my commandment, that you love one another as I have loved you. Greater love has no one than this, that someone lay down his life for his friends. You are my friends if you do what I command you. No longer do I call you servants, for the servant does not know what his master is doing; but I have called you friends, for all that I have heard from my Father I have made known to you."

Let's take a moment to meditate on His love for us. We were dead in our trespasses and sins. We were lost in our own self-centeredness. We were wicked in our selfish ambition. Jesus loved us in spite of ourselves. Now that Jesus has saved us, we still have continued to sin. We don't pursue Him like we should, but He pursues us. We're not faithful to Him like we should be, but He is faithful to us. We don't pray to Him like we should, but He mediates for us continually. We don't honor Him the way we should, but He always honors us. Jesus loves us in spite of ourselves. Even though we haven't earned His loyalty, Jesus says to us, "I will never leave you nor forsake you" (Hebrews 13:5).

You see, you can love your friends consistently because you have a divine Friend and Brother who loves you consistently. You can pour your life into your friends' lives because Jesus has poured His life into yours.

How exactly can your friendship with Jesus empower you to be a good friend to others?

_____

_____

_____

Third, you need to embrace the "**at all times**" aspect of friendship. "**At all times**" is another way of saying "for better, for worse; for richer, for poorer; in sickness and in health; till death do us part." True friendships are not fair-weather relationships. True friends celebrate with you when you succeed, help you up when you fall, and comfort you when you suffer. A friend is there when you get promoted and when you get fired. He is present when you win the championship and when go winless in your region. A friend is there when you're preparing for a first date and when you suffer a hard breakup. A friend is there when you have a birthday and when your parent dies. A friend is present when you're confused, discouraged, bitter, sick, or injured. A true friend doesn't run and hide when times are tough. As a matter of fact, when times are tough is when true friends step up to the plate and deliver.

At all times means at all times. Take a few minutes and think of two friends who have loved you at all times. Write their names down and offer a prayer of thanksgiving for their consistent friendship.

1. _____

_____

2. _____

_____

Fourth, loving your friends consistently involves some key elements. Here is a short list of how to be a consistent friend:

- Pray for them.

- Communicate with them.

- Speak truth to them.

- Forgive them.

- Bless them.

- Listen to them.

- Spend time with them.

Write down three of your closest friends. Your relationship to each of them is unique. So list the different ways you seek to be a good friend to each of them. If you see any shortfalls in your friendship, take this opportunity to commit yourself to a better exercise of friendship to them.

1. _____

_____

_____

2. _____

_____

_____

3. _____

_____

_____

▶ BE COURAGEOUS IN YOUR LOVE.

Courageous friendship is rising to the occasion to express God's love in the midst of adversity. A brother is born for adversity. **Born for** indicates purpose. The very reason a brother/friend is born is to minister during adversity. Anyone can be a fair-weather friend. The worth of a friendship is tested during adversity. Few people are willing to spend the time to help a friend with a personal problem.

Friends are courageous in times of **opposition**. William Wilberforce led a life-long campaign to abolish slave trade in England. He battled poor health, migraine headaches, fierce hostility, death threats, constant rejection, and slander. But what he had was a group of close friends who encouraged him, prayed for him, and rallied prayer support for him all over England. They surrounded him with their love and support. Don't let your friends stand alone, when they're standing for the glory of God.

Friends are courageous in times of **darkness**. My wife's mother died of cancer at a very young age. During the time of her suffering and death, my wife's friend Heather came over to the house and sat with Jamie numerous times. She just sat with my wife. This was encouraging, comforting, and courageous! Don't let your friends walk through darkness alone. Walk through the valley with them.

Friends are courageous in times of **failure**. We all fail a lot. We fail professionally, personally, morally, and relationally. A friend is someone who loves you in the failure and through the failure. The Apostle Peter failed in a huge way. He declared his undying loyalty to Jesus but then denied even knowing the Savior. Jesus didn't throw Peter aside or reject Peter. After His resurrection from the dead Jesus pulled Peter aside and graciously restored their relationship. Don't dismiss your friends in times of failure. Be there for them. Love them through it.

Friends are courageous in times of **sickness**. When we are sick, we are often at our weakest and most vulnerable state. Friends know that and seek to minister effectively during that time. I broke my two hands at different times while playing college baseball. I had two surgeries. I missed games and struggled emotionally. As I recovered, I did not receive a visit, phone call, or message. That hurt me. But it also taught me a lesson. Whenever your teammates or players are sick or injured it's a really good practice to communicate more with them than less.

I was in a bad car wreck some years ago. My friends were there for me in my time of adversity. My family was there in a matter of minutes and didn't leave my side until I was back on my feet. Two friends came over the night of the accident and sat with me. Another friend brought me a Chick-fil-a meal the next day. Another couple came and prayed for me. Another friend let me borrow his truck for more than two weeks. He spent hours searching the Internet to find the best deals for a replacement vehicle. I was so blessed in my time of adversity. I got to experience Proverbs 17:17, "A friend loves at all times, and a brother is born for adversity."

Friends are courageous in times of **crisis**. There is a great likelihood that just about all of us will go through a financial crisis in our lives. If you don't know the feeling of lying in bed at night, looking up at the ceiling, trying to figure out how to get out of the mess you're in financially, then count your blessings! A true friend recognizes a crisis and does whatever he or she can do to help alleviate stress and anxiety. When your friend has a crisis, then you have a crisis. A friend loves at all times, and a brother is born for adversity.

Consider the courageous friendship of Jonathan and David in 1 Samuel 20. Jonathan was the son of the king. If he stayed in his father's good graces, then he would likely experience the blessings of royalty the rest of his life. But David was his friend. And David was living for God's glory while Jonathan's father Saul was living for his own glory.

Read this chapter and observe how Jonathan showed courage in his friendship to David.

¹ Then David fled from Naioth in Ramah and came and said before Jonathan, "What have I done? What is my guilt? And what is my sin before your father, that he seeks my life?" ² And he said to him, "Far from it! You shall not die. Behold, my father does nothing either great or small without disclosing it to me. And why should my father hide this from me? It is not so." ³ But David vowed again, saying, "Your father knows well that I have found favor in your eyes, and he thinks, 'Do not let Jonathan know this, lest he be grieved.' But truly, as the LORD lives and as your soul lives, there is but a step between me and death." ⁴ Then Jonathan said to David, "Whatever you say, I will do for you." ⁵ David said to Jonathan, "Behold, tomorrow is the new moon, and I should not fail to sit at table with the king. But let me go, that I may hide myself in the field till the third day at evening. ⁶ If your father misses me at all, then say, 'David earnestly asked leave of me to run to Bethlehem his city, for there is a yearly sacrifice there for all the clan.' ⁷ If he says, 'Good!' it will be well with your servant, but if he is angry, then know that harm is determined by him. ⁸ Therefore deal kindly with your servant, for you have brought your servant into a covenant of the LORD with you. But if there is guilt in me, kill me yourself, for why should you bring me to your father?" ⁹ And Jonathan said, "Far be it from you! If I knew that it was determined by my father that harm should come to you, would I not tell you?" ¹⁰ Then David said to Jonathan, "Who will tell me if your father answers you roughly?" ¹¹ And Jonathan said to David, "Come, let us go out into the field." So they both went out into the field.

¹² And Jonathan said to David, "The LORD, the God of Israel, be witness! When I have sounded out my father, about this time tomorrow, or the third day, behold, if he is well disposed toward David, shall I not then send and disclose it to you? ¹³ But should it please my father to do you harm, the LORD do so to Jonathan and more also if I do not disclose it to you and send you away, that you may go in safety. May the LORD be with you, as he has been with my father. ¹⁴ If I am still alive, show me the steadfast love of the LORD, that I may not die; ¹⁵ and do not cut off your steadfast love from my house forever, when the LORD cuts off every one of the enemies of David from the face of the earth." ¹⁶ And Jonathan made a covenant with the house of David, saying, "May the LORD take vengeance on David's enemies." ¹⁷ And Jonathan made David swear again by his love for him, for he loved him as he loved his own soul.

¹⁸ Then Jonathan said to him, "Tomorrow is the new moon, and you will be missed, because your seat will be empty. ¹⁹ On the third day go down quickly to the place where you hid yourself when the matter was in hand, and remain beside the stone heap. ²⁰ And I will shoot three arrows to the side of it, as though I shot at a mark. ²¹ And behold, I will send the boy, saying, 'Go, find the arrows.' If I say to the boy, 'Look, the arrows are on this side of you, take them,' then you are to come, for, as the LORD lives, it is safe for you and there is no danger. ²² But if I say to the youth, 'Look, the arrows are beyond you,' then go, for the LORD has sent you away. ²³ And as for the matter of which you and I have spoken, behold, the LORD is between you and me forever."

²⁴ So David hid himself in the field. And when the new moon came, the king sat down to eat food. ²⁵ The king sat on his seat, as at other times, on the seat by the wall. Jonathan sat opposite, and Abner sat by Saul's side, but David's place was empty.

²⁶ Yet Saul did not say anything that day, for he thought, "Something has happened to him. He is not clean; surely he is not clean." ²⁷ But on the second day, the day after the new moon, David's place was empty. And Saul said to Jonathan his son, "Why has not the son of Jesse come to the meal, either yesterday or today?" ²⁸ Jonathan

answered Saul, "David earnestly asked leave of me to go to Bethlehem. ²⁹ He said, 'Let me go, for our clan holds a sacrifice in the city, and my brother has commanded me to be there. So now, if I have found favor in your eyes, let me get away and see my brothers.' For this reason he has not come to the king's table."

³⁰ Then Saul's anger was kindled against Jonathan, and he said to him, "You son of a perverse, rebellious woman, do I not know that you have chosen the son of Jesse to your own shame, and to the shame of your mother's nakedness? ³¹ For as long as the son of Jesse lives on the earth, neither you nor your kingdom shall be established. Therefore send and bring him to me, for he shall surely die." ³² Then Jonathan answered Saul his father, "Why should he be put to death? What has he done?" ³³ But Saul hurled his spear at him to strike him. So Jonathan knew that his father was determined to put David to death. ³⁴ And Jonathan rose from the table in fierce anger and ate no food the second day of the month, for he was grieved for David, because his father had disgraced him.

³⁵ In the morning Jonathan went out into the field to the appointment with David, and with him a little boy. ³⁶ And he said to his boy, "Run and find the arrows that I shoot." As the boy ran, he shot an arrow beyond him. ³⁷ And when the boy came to the place of the arrow that Jonathan had shot, Jonathan called after the boy and said, "Is not the arrow beyond you?" ³⁸ And Jonathan called after the boy, "Hurry! Be quick! Do not stay!" So Jonathan's boy gathered up the arrows and came to his master. ³⁹ But the boy knew nothing. Only Jonathan and David knew the matter. ⁴⁰ And Jonathan gave his weapons to his boy and said to him, "Go and carry them to the city." ⁴¹ And as soon as the boy had gone, David rose from beside the stone heap and fell on his face to the ground and bowed three times. And they kissed one another and wept with one another, David weeping the most. ⁴² Then Jonathan said to David, "Go in peace, because we have sworn both of us in the name of the LORD, saying, 'The LORD shall be between me and you, and between my offspring and your offspring, forever.' " And he rose and departed, and Jonathan went into the city.

What impresses you about Jonathan and David's friendship?

_____

_____

_____

_____

_____

_____

What kind of inspiration do you feel in your own friendships as you see these two friends' courage in adversity?

_____

_____

_____

_____

_____

_____

How can you become a better friend to your teammates so they can understand what it means to be a good friend?

_____

_____

_____

_____

_____

_____

GAME CHANGER

"A man of many companions may come to ruin, but there is a friend who sticks closer than a brother." – Proverbs 18:24

"Greater love has no one than this, that someone lay down his life for his friends." – John 15:13

Jesus died for His enemies to make them His friends. He is the most faithful friend. He laid down His life for us. He sticks so close that He never leaves us, turns His back on us, or abandons us. No matter what. Consider the message of the great hymn, *Great is Thy Faithfulness*.

Great is Thy Faithfulness, O God my Father.

There is no shadow of turning with Thee;

Thou changest not, Thy compassions, they fail not.

As Thou hast been, Thou forever wilt be.

Great is Thy faithfulness!

Great is Thy faithfulness!

Morning by morning new mercies I see;

All I have needed Thy hand hath provided –

Great is Thy faithfulness, Lord, unto me

Summer and winter, and springtime and harvest,

Sun, moon and stars in their courses above,

Join with all nature in manifold witness

To Thy great faithfulness, mercy and love.

Pardon for sin and a peace that endureth,

Thine own dear presence to cheer and to guide;

Strength for today and bright hope for tomorrow,

Blessings all mine, with ten thousand beside!

ONE BIG THING

What is the most significant lesson for you to take with you from this chapter?

_____

_____

_____

_____

_____

_____

_____

IMPACT PRAYER

Father in heaven, friendship is a gift from heaven. Thank You for giving us the opportunity to experience love, loyalty, and joy in relationships with others. Please help us be good friends and to experience the life-long blessings of loyal love. In the name of Jesus. Amen.

NOTES

★ ★ ★

CHAPTER NINE
DISCERNING ATHLETES
AVOID ADDICTION

PROVERBS 23:29-35

STUDY STARTER

When we're honest with ourselves, we must admit that we all have problems. We have problems with our health, finances, relationships, sports, family, and more. But one of the problems that we can be unable to see or unwilling to admit is our inclination toward addictions. **Every single one of us has the capacity to be addicted to something.** For some it may be alcohol, illegal drugs, prescription drugs, or painkillers. For others it may be cigarettes, coffee, sweet tea, food, gambling, or sex. We can even be addicted to control, attention, or approval.

The human heart is hard-wired for satisfaction and allegiance. We will not cease our pursuit of satisfaction until we get it. Once we get it, we will be unflinchingly loyal to it, until something else lures us away with its promises of deeper satisfaction.

At the 2015 CMA Awards Show Justin Timberlake and Chris Stapleton sang together. These are the lyrics to their song Tennessee Whiskey:

> I used to spend my nights out in a barroom
>
> Liquor was the only love I've known
>
> But you rescued me from reaching for the bottle
>
> And you brought me back from being too far gone
>
> You're as smooth as Tennessee whiskey
>
> You're as sweet as strawberry wine
>
> You're as warm as a glass of brandy
>
> And I stay stoned on your love all the time
>
> I look for love in all the same old places
>
> Found the bottom of the bottle always dry
>
> But when you poured out your heart, I didn't waste it
>
> 'Cause there nothing like your love to gettin' me high
>
> You're as smooth as Tennessee whiskey
>
> You're as sweet as strawberry wine
>
> You're as warm as a glass of brandy
>
> And I stay stoned on your love all the time.
>
> I stay stoned on your love all the time

Their performance has been viewed on YouTube over 482,000,000 times. Check the zeros. That's 482 million! Why is that song so wildly popular? I think for two reasons. First, their musical performance was incredible! Second, people resonate with the joy of satisfaction and the excruciating pain of losing it. We are all hardwired for satisfaction! We won't stop until we get it. And when we lose it, we'll find something or someone to replace it. Let this truth sink deep into your heart. **We all have the potential to be addicted, because we all have longings to be satisfied.**

What is addiction? Wikipedia defines it as "a state characterized by compulsive engagement in rewarding stimuli, despite adverse consequences. The two properties that characterize all addictive stimuli are that they are reinforcing and intrinsically rewarding." Let's study Proverbs 23:29-35 to gain God's perspective on addiction and how we can find freedom from it.

STUDY PASSAGE

[29] Who has woe? Who has sorrow?

Who has strife? Who has complaining?

Who has wounds without cause? Who has redness of eyes?

[30] Those who tarry long over wine;

those who go to try mixed wine.

[31] Do not look at wine when it is red,

when it sparkles in the cup

and goes down smoothly.

[32] In the end it bites like a serpent

and stings like an adder.

[33] Your eyes will see strange things,

and your heart utter perverse things.

[34] You will be like one who lies down in the midst of the sea,

like one who lies on the top of a mast.

[35] "They struck me," you will say, "but I was not hurt;

they beat me, but I did not feel it.

When shall I awake?

I must have another drink."

STUDY HELP

29-30 Questions about Addiction

- "**woe**" = impassioned expression of grief and despair or anger and disgust.
- "**sorrow**" = deep distress caused by disappointment or dissatisfaction.
- "**strife**" = bitter conflict, disagreement.
- "**complaining**" = expression of dissatisfaction.
- "**wounds** without cause" = bruises, injuries without explanation.
- "**redness of eyes**" = dullness of eyes, as in drunken eyes.
- "**tarry**" = linger, delay, remain behind.
- "**wine**" = beverage made from fermented grape juice. Fermentation is the metabolic process that converts sugar to acids, gases, or alcohol. Grain is fermented to produce beer. Grapes are fermented to produce wine.
- "**go**" = search out, pursue.
- "**mixed wine**" = possibly with honey and spices. The goal here is to make wine more spicy and potent than it already is.

31-34 Warnings against Addiction

- "**serpent**" = snake.
- "**adder**" = poisonous snake.
- "**utter**" = speak.
- "**perverse**" = rebellious, twisted, unholy.
- "**midst**" = heart.
- "**mast**" = the tall upright post on a boat that carries the sail.

- **"They struck me,"** you will say, **"but I was not hurt; they beat me, but I did not feel it."** Alcohol softens pain in an unhelpful way. If you don't feel pain, there is no motivation to remove yourself from the source of the pain. Sadly, there will be plenty of pain once the anesthetic wears off.

- **"When shall I awake? I must have another drink."** = The tragedy of addiction is that despite the horrible experience of being drunk, once the drunkard sobers up there is a frantic search for the next drink. "I must have another drink" is the life verse of addicts. This proverb describes more than a single night's drinking and a morning's hangover. It describes the increasingly degenerative effects of the addict.

STUDY QUESTIONS

1. What are the six markers of one who tarries over wine and drinks mixed wine (verse 29)?

_____

_____

_____

_____

_____

2. Even though wine is appealing and attractive, it is very dangerous. According to verses 32-34 it will carry out an attack on you. What does wine have the power to do?

_____

_____

_____

_____

_____

_____

3. In the drunkard's testimony from verse 35 he makes two boasts, asks one question, and makes one demand. Write those down.

1) Boasts:

_____

_____

2) Question:

_____

_____

3) Demand:

_____

_____

4. Read through the passage again (vv. 29-35). What thoughts do you have about the process of intoxication and addiction?

_____

_____

_____

_____

5. This proverb specifically uses wine as the agent of intoxication and addiction. What else can person be intoxicated with and addicted to?

_____

_____

_____

_____

STUDY SUMMARY

Addiction is a consuming slavery to an artificial god. But the Gospel transforms people to the freedom and joy of worshiping the one true God.

ATHLETE CONNECTION

As a discerning athlete you will know the dangers of addiction and train yourself to navigate away from enslavement to anything that distracts you from worship. You will also warn your teammates of addiction and point them to real satisfaction in Christ.

KEYS TO WINNING

▶ **VIDEO GUIDE AT KINGDOMSPORTS.ONLINE**

▶ UNDERSTAND THE PLUMMET OF ADDICTION.

This passage graphically describes the descent of addiction. It paints a frightening picture of addiction's grip. Addicts cry "woe" and experience sorrow because of the pain that addiction brings to their lives. Addicts get into fights that leave bruises because they lose all sense of proper behavior. They say and do the wrong thing at the wrong time and they get into trouble. They do not see clearly, think clearly, or act rightly.

What does addiction do? It poisons and kills you. It disorients and disengages you. It sickens and staggers you. Wine looks so enticing, so good. The drink goes down the throat so smoothly, but the consequences are disastrous. Wine is like the poisonous bite of a snake. It can kill. But before it kills, it disorients and disengages all sense of wisdom.

The progression of addiction goes like this: sight of wine, captivation with wine, pursuit of wine, indulgence of wine, disorientation, depraved speech, numbness, enslavement, destruction, fractured relationships, broken lives. *Addiction takes you farther than you wanted to go, keeps you longer than you wanted to stay, and costs you more than you wanted to pay.*

The descending plunge of Addiction is this:

- I don't like the way I feel.

- I want to manage my world my way.

- I like this. This is what I have been looking for. I want to keep doing this!

- This means so much to me. I love it. I want more.

- I NEED more. This is my god.

- This hurts. I've been betrayed. I want it, but I don't want it.

How can you know if you or someone you love is addicted to something?

- If you're satisfied when you get it, but anxious and desperate when you don't get it, you're likely addicted.

- If you're happy and calm when you get it, but irritable and angry when you don't get it, you're likely addicted.

- If you're defensive and argumentative when people approach you and try to help you, you're likely addicted.

- If you find greater excitement and peace with it than you do in worshiping God and serving others, then you're likely addicted.

This proverb leaves us asking the question, "How can I escape the destructive pattern and fatal results of addiction?"

In your own words, describe your experience with addiction or addicts. What pattern have you experienced or witnessed? What destructive results have you seen?

1) Pattern

_____

_____

_____

_____

_____

2) Results

_____

_____

_____

_____

▸ EMBRACE THE POWER OVER ADDICTION.

Apart from the Gospel we all have a story. And it's not a good one. In the garden, Adam chose the forbidden fruit over the faithful God. In the wilderness, Israel chose a golden calf over the Lord of glory. On the rooftop David chose adultery over fidelity. In the darkness, Peter chose denial over allegiance. Their story isn't divorced from our story. Their story is our story. We are sinners just like they were. We have all rebelled against the goodness and holiness of God.

But God is in the business of re-writing our story! Jesus Christ, the eternal Son of God, came to planet earth on a mission. He fasted for 40 days and was hungry. Then He was tempted in a significant way. Satan approached Him and tempted Him with the pleasure of food, the pride of authority, and the power of a kingdom. (see Luke 4:1-13)

Jesus was tempted to engage in idolatry. The temptation was real and appealing. Imagine how hungry He must have been. But Jesus stood against the temptation with the authority of God's Word and the power of the Holy Spirit. And the beautiful truth is that His victory has become your victory. His success has become your success. His record has become your record. Since He won, you win!

You see, after His temptation Jesus ultimately experienced the cross. The cross says that the kingdom of darkness no longer has power over you. The cross paid your way out of Satan's domain. The cross says that the penalty for your sin has been paid. The cross says that your sins are forgiven. The cross is the place where your sins and sicknesses are healed. The cross says that Jesus has done it all. The cross has guaranteed hope and joy for those who put their trust in Jesus.

No addiction is so powerful that it can't be broken by the power of the cross. The Gospel breaks the power of addictions and reveals the emptiness of the promises they make. The power of the Gospel is stronger than the power of addiction. The satisfaction of the Gospel is better than the satisfaction of addiction. The outcome of the Gospel is better than the outcome of addiction.

In addiction you're looking for an escape, in Jesus you find a home.

In addiction you're looking for rescue, in Jesus you find redemption.

In addiction you're looking for a temporary thrill, in Jesus you find ultimate fulfillment.

Adam, Israel, and David were looking for a temporary thrill. Let's learn from their empty experience and run to Christ. He has the power to free us from our addictions and satisfy us with an unending, joy-producing satisfaction that will only increase day by day as we walk with Him.

Describe your personal experience with Jesus. What has the Gospel done for you in the area of daily satisfaction and peace?

_____

_____

_____

_____

_____

_____

_____

You will be tempted toward addiction of some kind. So will your teammates. They may even have parents or siblings who are addicted now. How can you leverage your personal relationship with Jesus to bring hope and help to their situations?

_____

_____

_____

_____

_____

_____

_____

▶ ESTABLISH A PLAN TO FIGHT ADDICTION.

Every battle needs a good battle plan. Consider an army that is facing the most critical battle of the war. A concerned soldier asks, "General, what is your plan?" The General replies, "Well, I thought we would have a late breakfast, then engage the enemy." Alarmed, the soldier asks, "But what is your plan?" The General cluelessly replies, "That is my plan." That's a plan for failure!!! If you fail to plan, then you plan to fail. That is especially true with addiction.

Let me offer a battle plan to fight addiction.

- **Remember the cross**. The cross is where you find forgiveness, love, confidence, satisfaction, and glory.

- **Own your identity**. You are a son or daughter in the Father's arms, not a victim in the devil's hands. You are a worshiper of God, not an idolater. You are a warrior in God's army, not a helpless victim of the devil's devices. You are an ambassador for King Jesus, not a minion in Satan's empire of darkness.

- **Practice spiritual disciplines**. These are the means of grace that God's people have been using for centuries.

  - Read the Bible. See your small story in God's big story.

  - Pray consistently throughout the day.

  - Sing songs of victory to God.

  - Journal your spiritual journey.

  - Gather with God's people for worship.

  - Listen intently to preaching.

  - Celebrate the Lord's Supper.

  - Fellowship with God's people.

  - Serve others.

  - Pray for others.

- **Change your thought-patterns**. Don't savor your addiction in your mind. This is a huge mistake. God cares as much about who you are on the inside as He does about what you do on the outside. He wants your heart, mind, and strength. So put away thoughts about your addiction and put on thoughts about Him.

- **Set up boundaries**. Create barriers that will prevent you from getting close to your addiction. Include people to hold you accountable and give you encouragement. Find a faithful friend who will walk with you and help you in this fight.

- **Get off the mat**. When you get knocked down, don't stay down. Get up! If a relapse happens, it's easy to give up and go back to where you started. After falling into the addiction again, it is rare for someone to stop at only one pill, drink, internet site, or whatever. One more leads to one more. Don't be deceived. There is hope even after a relapse. There is forgiveness and power. But you must believe the promises of God and disbelieve the lies of the enemy. Get up! Self-pity will destroy you. No addiction has more power than the Gospel. Trust God. And go be with God's people. You will find hope and help there.

As an athlete you know all about creating a game plan for victory. You know how to identify your own team's weaknesses and strengths. You also know how to identify your opponent's advantages and disadvantages. You're good at creating mismatches that favor your team. If one of your teammates were to approach you and confess that he has developed an addiction and asks you to personally help him and hold him accountable, what kind of plan would you help him put in place?

_____

_____

_____

_____

_____

_____

_____

_____

If you know that one of your teammates is addicted to playing video games, how will you handle that situation? You can tell that it clearly affects his academic, athletic, and social life. He has bragged to teammates about how he regularly stays up until 3:00 am gaming. You've noticed that he no longer hangs out with his teammates. His GPA has dropped drastically. His performance at practice and games is nowhere near what he did last season. What are you going to do in that situation?

_____

_____

_____

_____

_____

GAME CHANGER

New Jersey Governor Chris Christie lost one of his law-school friends to addiction. It impacted him deeply. Christie's friend was an Ivy League university graduate and a Seton Hall Law School graduate. He was the first to get a great job, the first to make $1 million, and the first to make partner at a law firm. He married a beautiful wife, had three beautiful children, and was in perfect physical condition. He had a big house, nice cars, and went on great vacations.

He suffered a back injury while running. He felt pain. So he took Percocet. Over time he developed an addiction. His enslavement to medicine was destructive to him and everyone around him. Intervention was attempted. It failed. He lost his wife, kids, house, cars, job, law license, driver's license, savings, and retirement. At age 52 he was found dead in a hotel room with an empty bottle of Percocet and an empty quart of vodka by his side. This is what Governor Christie said about his friend, "He couldn't get help. Now he's dead. It can happen to anyone. We must be able to treat them. We must give them the tools they need to get better."

This is a tragic story. And Mr. Christie is right. It can happen to anyone. But just as addiction can happen to anyone, so can redemption. Jesus Christ is the ultimate Game Changer when it comes to addiction. He has the power to pull a person out of slavery into freedom, away from despair into joy. It's not an easy road. But it is an open road that leads to true rest. Anyone can take it. That's why He said, "Come to me, all who labor and are heavy laden, and I will give you rest. Take my yoke upon you, and learn from me, for I am gentle and lowly in heart, and you will find rest for your souls. For my yoke is easy, and my burden is light."

We grieve over those who are under the power of addiction. And we pray that they will experience redemption through the Gospel of Jesus Christ. It is the power of God unto salvation for all who believe.

ONE BIG THING

What is the most significant lesson for you to take with you from this chapter?

_____

_____

_____

_____

_____

_____

_____

IMPACT PRAYER

Father in heaven, without Your guidance and help we will fall prey to the seducing power of addiction. Please strengthen us to find our identity, hope, and joy at Your feet. Give us increasing joy as we worship You. In the great name of Jesus, we pray. Amen.

★ ★ ★

CHAPTER TEN
DISCERNING ATHLETES
LIVE FEARLESSLY

PROVERBS 29:25

STUDY STARTER

On the night that Jesus was betrayed He was also denied. The disciple who pledged complete loyalty to Him denied Him not once or twice, but three times in the same night. How could that happen? Because in that moment He feared the rejection and ridicule of men.

Six weeks later Act 2 and 3 described how that same disciple stood in front of thousands of hostile people and boldly proclaimed, "Men of Israel, hear these words: Jesus of Nazareth, a man attested to you by God with mighty works and wonders and signs that God did through Him in your midst, as you yourselves know—this Jesus, delivered up according to the definite plan and foreknowledge of God, you crucified and killed by the hands of lawless men. God raised him up, loosing the pangs of death, because it was not possible for him to be held by it…. Let all the house of Israel therefore know for certain that God has made Him both Lord and Christ… Repent and be baptized everyone of you in the name of Jesus Christ for the forgiveness of your sins, and you will receive the gift of the Holy Spirit." How was he able to be so fearless? Because in that moment he fully trusted in the Lord.

A few days later, after 3,000 people had repented and believed in Jesus through his preaching, and after a crippled man was healed at the Temple, he was arrested by the religious leaders and cross-examined by the Jewish elite. They asked him, "By what power or by what name did you do this?" Being full of the Holy Spirit he replied, "Let it be known to all of you and to all the people of Israel that by the name of Jesus Christ of Nazareth, whom you crucified, whom God raised from the dead—by Him this man is standing before you well. This Jesus is the stone that was rejected by you, the builders, which has become the cornerstone. And there is salvation in no one else, for there is no other name under heaven given among men by which we must be saved." So they charged him not to speak or teach at all in the name of Jesus. And he replied, "We cannot but speak of what we have seen and heard." How was he able to be so fearless? Because in that moment he fully trusted in the Lord.

Years later, after the church of Jesus Christ had exploded in growth and spread throughout the Roman Empire, this same man ate and drank with Gentile Christians. He enjoyed their company, worshiped with them, laughed with them, and benefited from them. But when Jews from Jerusalem traveled to see him, he withdrew from his Gentile friends and would not publicly eat with them or really have anything to do with them. How could he so easily turn his back on his friends? Because in that moment he feared the disapproval of his Jewish brothers.

Who am I referring to? Peter, of course. Peter is one of the big guns of Christianity! He is the rock upon whom Jesus Christ built the early church. But if you look at his life, it is a mixed bag of fearing man and trusting in the Lord. Are you and I not the exact same way? Are we not the perfect contradiction of trusting in the Lord on Sunday and fearing the rejection of men on Monday? Athlete, allow me to encourage you. God knows you're going to fail. He knows you're going to have problems with fearing man. And He's not going to kick you out of His kingdom when you do. He is simply going to extend His grace and help you trust Him more and more every day. Let's study Proverbs 29:25 with confidence that He is going to deepen our faith and create within us a spirit of fearlessness for the glory of His name.

STUDY PASSAGE

^{25} The fear of man lays a snare,

but whoever trusts in the LORD is safe.

STUDY HELP

- "**fear**" = trembling, anxiety, fear. In 1 Samuel 14:15 Jonathan invaded the Philistine army camp. This is what Samuel says happened, "And there was a panic in the camp, in the field, and among all the people. The garrison and even the raiders trembled, the earth quaked, and it became a very great panic." They were afraid. They trembled. They panicked. Turns out, it was just Jonathan and his armor bearer. But their own fear overtook them and brought demise.
- "**of man**" = people.
- "**The fear of man**" is a phrase that means an unhealthy reverence for people. It is a craving for people's acceptance and approval.

- "**lays**" = sets, positions.

- "**a snare**" = a trap, primarily used for entangling animals.

- "**trust**" = to fully rely on the integrity, strength, and ability of a person or a thing.

- "**is safe**" = is inaccessibly high. Picture an ancient city that sits on top of a very high mountain. On one side of the mountain is a steep cliff. On the other side of the mountain is difficult terrain, thick brush, bears, mountain lions, and all kinds of wild animals. The person who lives in that city is safe from attack. Why? Because he lives safely on top of the mountain. No one can attack him because he is inaccessibly high and guarded by the natural barriers that surround his city. In the same way, whoever fully relies on the Lord is inaccessible.

STUDY QUESTIONS

1. What does the fear of man do?

_____

_____

_____

2. What is so dangerous about fearing people?

_____

_____

_____

3. Who gets to experience safety in this life?

_____

_____

_____

4. What does it mean to trust in the Lord?

_____

_____

_____

5. Who has made the biggest impact on you because of their trust in the Lord? Explain.

_____

_____

_____

6. How can it be safe to trust in the Lord when so many people in the world are hostile toward those who trust in Him? Consider the experiences of Hagar in Genesis 16:7-14, Esther in Esther 1-10, Naomi and Ruth in Ruth 1-4.

_____

_____

_____

_____

_____

_____

STUDY SUMMARY

Even though it looks and feels safe, the fear of man is the most dangerous way to live your life. And even though it looks and feels dangerous, trusting the LORD with all that you are and have is the safest way to live your life.

ATHLETE CONNECTION

Who does God use the most in this life? God uses leaders who don't find their identity or worth in the approval of others, but in Jesus Christ. He uses leaders who live each day trusting in Him for great things. The discerning athlete will not fear man but trust in the Lord.

KEYS TO WINNING

▶ VIDEO GUIDE AT KINGDOMSPORTS.ONLINE

▶ DECREASE YOUR FEAR.

"The fear of man lays a snare."

Picture with me a hunter who uses a metal snare with big, sharp teeth on it. He sets the snare on the ground and covers it with leaves and grass. He ties one end of a rope to it and the other end he ties to the tree. His plan is to trap a bear. He walks away from the trap. But then he realizes he left his cell phone laying by the tree. In a moment of haste, he runs back to grab the phone, when all of a sudden, he steps right into the snare. The sharp teeth penetrate into his leg. The pulley-action of the rope does its job. And now the hunter is hanging upside down from a tree. He is bleeding profusely from his leg. And unless a miracle happens, he is hopelessly destined to die all alone in the woods by the trap he himself set.

That's the picture Proverbs 29:25 is painting. The fear of man is a trap that many people set for themselves and then fall into. And once they do, it is nearly impossible to escape.

So what is the fear of man? The fear of man is the worship of being accepted and approved by people. It is the attempt to live your life in such a way that people will accept you and approve of you. It is marked by a continual desire for others' acceptance and a controlling fear of their rejection.

The fear of man can be expressed in **worship**. A Christian may want to raise her hands while singing praises to the Lord, but she is concerned that her family or friends will think she is too radical. So she suppresses that urge and folds her hands behind her back.

The fear of man can be expressed in **friendship**. A player may know that he needs to address a serious matter with his teammate, but he is afraid the teammate will reject him if he does. So he remains silent while his teammate makes bad decisions that can hurt himself and the team.

The fear of man can be expressed in **missions**. A Christian may want to share the Gospel with her non-Christian co-worker, but she is afraid it will make their relationship weird after that. So she keeps their relationship on the level of talking about the weather, music, and art.

The fear of man is like a dictator. It sovereignly rules over your life and decision-making with no concern for what will glorify God or produce joy in you.

The fear of man is like a noose. It slowly but surely squeezes the life out of you. Before long, the person God created you to be no longer even exists, but now a puppet exists. And the people around you pull the strings so that you speak, act, perform in the way they want you to.

The fear of man is like a vacuum. Joy is the inner delight of trusting God and being accepted by God. When you fear man you no longer have that delight. It is sucked out of you by the constant concern for being accepted and approved by men.

Who can fall victim to the fear of man? Anyone. Athletes often want and need other athletes' approval. Players often want and need fans' approval.

These questions will help diagnose if you have a problem with fearing man:

- Do you ask yourself, "I wonder what so-and-so will think if I do this?"
- Do you regularly second-guess yourself because of what others might think?
- Are you afraid of making mistakes that'll make you look bad before others?
- Are you easily embarrassed?
- Do you ever lie, just to make yourself look better in people's eyes?
- Do other people often make you angry or depressed?
- Do you try your very best to be better than other people?
- Do you try your best to be wealthier than other people?
- Skinnier than other people?
- Stronger than other people?
- More beautiful than other people?

Let me tell you about the drive to succeed. If your goal is not God's glory, then your desire for success is rooted in the fear of man. It just doesn't look like fear. It looks like confidence or assurance. But at its very core, it is worshiping the acceptance and approval of people.

Why do we fear people? Because they can expose and humiliate us. They can reject, ridicule, or despise us. They can attack, oppress, or threaten us. And those possibilities effectively dominate us when we see people as more significant and powerful than God.

Apart from the Gospel, we will be afraid of being exposed for who we really are. We will fear exposure. Because of that we will try our very best to find acceptance and approval from men without having our weaknesses exposed. We will set up our whole lives in such a way that pursues the admiration of others. We will go places, do things, say things, avoid things, wear certain clothes, and drive certain cars to gain people's acceptance. But when we find our identity and approval in the Gospel, then we no longer need men's approval because we have God's.

Where does the fear of man lead to? It leads you away from the increasing joy of knowing God to the increasing anxiety of needing the acceptance and approval of people.

You should know these things about the fear of man:

- You will never be able to please everyone.

- You will always disappoint some people.

- You will never be good enough for some people.

- You will always be a step-behind or a notch-below their acceptance.

- If you judge the quality of your life by the acceptance and approval of the people around you, then you will never find the unceasing joy and abundant life that Jesus came to give you.

- The only acceptance and approval that matters are the Lord's. If you didn't find acceptance and approval in Him here on earth, then you will not find it in Him then. You see, wherever you find your rest in this life will also be where you will find it in the life to come.

If you know you have a problem with fearing man, this is how you can repent:

- See it – the first thing you must do is see your fear of man.

- Feel Sorrow for it – your heart is grieved because you have offended God.

- Confess it – Confession is saying the same thing about your sin that God says about it.

- Turn from it – your heart must turn from fear of man to love for Christ. Repentance is always accompanied by faith in Christ.

How does the fear of man most often reveal itself in your heart?

_____

_____

_____

_____

Are you able to identify the fear of man in your heart when you're experiencing it?

What do you normally do about it?

_____

_____

_____

_____

How do your athletes demonstrate the fear of man?

_____

_____

_____

_____

▸ INCREASE YOUR FAITH.

"but whoever trusts in the LORD is safe."

What does it really mean to "trust in the Lord"? It means that you believe He is, who the Bible says He is, that He is for you and not against you, that He is infinitely powerful, infinitely wise, and infinitely good.

In 2003 I was five years into ministry with FCA. I was almost 28 years old and God was giving me more Gospel-preaching opportunities in a week than most people get in a lifetime. But there was a slight problem. I was untrained in the Gospel. I didn't go to Bible school. I didn't go to seminary. I had never taken a teaching or preaching class at church. I had never even been in a serious Bible study until that year. Yet, I was regularly preaching, teaching, and counseling. I needed to be trained!

So my wife and I moved 2,000 miles away for me to attend The Master's Seminary. I was scared and intimidated. At our orientation I looked around and surrounding me was a bunch of 22-year-old glasses-wearing, laptop-toting, Bible-degree holding, smart guys. Here I was, five or six years older than them, a three-ring binder in my hand, a guy from a small town in Alabama, a jock. Some guys sat next to me just so they could hear me talk in my Southern drawl.

My very first class was Hebrew grammar. I had to learn a language that is printed right to left. Everything is backwards and much harder to learn. At some point one of the former students came to class and gave testimony about how he did his morning devotions in the Hebrew language. I was so intimidated. I thought, "What in the world have I done?!? I have left everything I own. I have left my ministry. Jamie has left her job. We have left our families, our church, our friends. We have left everything that is "safe." And I'm absolutely clueless as to whether or not I can pass a single class.

I don't know if you've ever felt in-over-your-head. But I want to tell you I have never been more scared or intimidated in my life. The first month of school I battled a spiritual darkness that I've never felt. I had a lot of unbelief. But at the very same time, I've never felt more alive or more excited. Why? Because it was one of the first times in my life where I was in a position that if God didn't come through, I was toast!

Well, God did come through. God did sustain me. God did give me everything I needed. God did deliver me through some very dark days. Even though it felt dangerous, the safest place I could have been was exactly where I was: in the trustworthy arms of my faithful God.

You may be in a position where you need to step out in faith and trust God with the results. Let me tell you this. There is more safety in failing for God than succeeding for men. Think of a time that you didn't trust God. How did that turn out for you? Think of a time that you stepped out in faith and trusted God. How did that turn out? The only acceptance and approval you need is what you already have in Jesus Christ.

Why don't we trust God more than we do? Because we don't know Him well, study Him much, or spend time with Him in prayer. The more time we spend with God, the more we trust Him. The less time we spend with God, the less we trust Him. Leonard Ravenhill once said, "The Christian who is intimate with God will never be intimidated by men."

List 5 character traits of God that make Him trustworthy.

1)_____

_____

2)_____

_____

3)_____

_____

4)_____

_____

5)_____

_____

List 5 accomplishments of God that make Him trustworthy.

1)_____

_____

2)_____

_____

3)_____

_____

4)_____

_____

5)_____

_____

List two ways in which you need to step out in faith and trust the Lord today.

1)_____

_____

2)_____

_____

GAME CHANGER

Jesus did not cower to the fear of man, even in the most terrifying moments of His life. Instead, He entrusted Himself to His Father because He knew the safest place He could be is in the strong arms of His Father.

Jesus is a Game Changer for us. He came to die for us. He came to purchase our eternal acceptance before God. And He was successful in that attempt. So we don't need man's approval. We have God's approval. And no one is more important than God. His approval trumps everyone else's. And through the shedding of Christ's blood, we have God's approval signed, sealed, and delivered.

Jesus lived fearlessly to establish God's kingdom.

We can live fearlessly to expand God's kingdom.

ONE BIG THING

What is the most significant lesson for you to take with you from this chapter?

_____

_____

_____

_____

_____

_____

_____

IMPACT PRAYER

Father in heaven, You are infinitely wise and discerning. Thank You for loving us so much that You would reveal Your way of wisdom to us. Please help us prioritize, pursue, and enjoy wisdom so that we can truly lead others toward You. In the name of Jesus, Amen.

CONCLUSION

These are the titles of each chapter you studied. Circle the two that carried the most significance to you in your pursuit of God's wisdom.

Week 1   Discerning Athletes VALUE WISDOM

Week 2   Discerning Athletes TRUST IN THE LORD

Week 3   Discerning Athletes CHOOSE THE RIGHT PATH

Week 4   Discerning Athletes WORK DILIGENTLY

Week 5   Discerning Athletes SPEAK WORDS OF LIFE

Week 6   Discerning Athletes WALK HUMBLY

Week 7   Discerning Athletes BLESS THEIR CITIES

Week 8   Discerning Athletes MODEL FRIENDSHIP

Week 9   Discerning Athletes AVOID ADDICTION

Week 10   Discerning Athletes LIVE FEARLESSLY

Take this opportunity to write out a prayer to God that articulates your desire to be a discerning athlete who lives with His wisdom and discernment. Especially ask Him to help you grow in skill in the two areas you circled above.

_____

_____

_____

Write down the names and descriptions of the people who participated in this study with you so that you can remember them and the contribution they made to your spiritual growth.

_____

_____

_____

www.ingramcontent.com/pod-product-compliance
Lightning Source LLC
La Vergne TN
LVHW051240080426
835513LV00016B/1698